Published in Great Britain in 2007 by Wiley-Academy, a division of John Wiley & Sons Ltd

Second Edition Copyright © 2007 John Wiley & Sons Ltd, The Atrium, Southern Gate, Chichester,

West Sussex PO19 8SQ, England

Telephone   (+44) 1243 779777

Email (for orders and customer service enquiries): cs-books@wiley.co.uk

Visit our Home Page on www.wiley.com

Anniversary Logo Design: Richard Pacifico

Other Wiley Editorial Offices

John Wiley & Sons Inc., 111 River Street, Hoboken, NJ 07030, USA

Jossey-Bass, 989 Market Street, San Francisco, CA 94103-1741, USA

Wiley-VCH Verlag GmbH, Boschstr. 12, D-69469 Weinheim, Germany

John Wiley & Sons Australia Ltd, 42 McDougall Street, Milton, Queensland 4064, Australia

John Wiley & Sons (Asia) Pte Ltd, 2 Clementi Loop #02-01, Jin Xing Distripark, Singapore 129809

John Wiley & Sons Canada Ltd, 5353 Dundas Street West, Suite 400, Etobicoke, Ontario M9B 6H8

Wiley also publishes its books in a variety of electronic formats. Some content that appears in print may not be available in electronic books.

Executive Commissioning Editor: Helen Castle

Content Editor: Louise Porter

Publishing Assistant: Calver Lezama

ISBN 978 0 470 06647 8

Cover design from Lotte, Seoul by Universal Design Studio

Page design and layouts by Liz Sephton, UK

Printed and bound by Conti Tipocolor, Italy

Fashion Retail

2nd Edition

Eleanor Curtis & Howard Watson   Series Designer Liz Sephton

contents

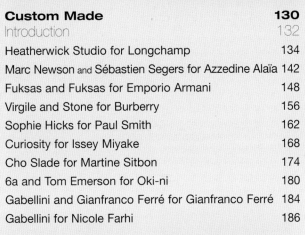

We would like to acknowledge the following for assistance with the two editions of this book: Helen Castle of Wiley-Academy for her interest, constructive comments and helpful suggestions; also at Wiley-Academy, Louise Porter, Mariangela Palazzi-Williams; Caroline Ellerby, Famida Rasheed and Abigail Grater for their editorial work; Liz Sephton for the design; Matteo Piazza and all other photographers, architects, designers and their assistants and representatives who have answered our requests and provided us with material for the book.

Acknowledgements

The authors and publisher gratefully acknowledge the following for permission to reproduce material in the book. While every effort has been made to contact copyright holders for their permission to reprint material in this book the publishers would be grateful to hear from any copyright holder who is not acknowledged here and will undertake to rectify any errors or omissions in future editions.

Cover: © Universal Design Studio

pp 1, 212-17 © Jordan Mozer and Associates, Ltd; pp 2-3, 4(r), 15(b), 76-81, 122-9, 196-203 © Universal Design Studio; pp 4(l), 60-1, 66-7, 82-4, 86-92, 156-61 photos: © Matteo Piazza; pp 5(tl), 134-40 photos: © Nikolas Koenig; pp 5(bl), 142-6, 147(tl+tr) photos: © Christoph Kicherer; pp 5(r), 9, 204-11 photos: © Diephotodesigner.de; p 10(tl+tr) © Leon Chew; p 10(bl+br) © Tom Emerson; p 11 © Bulgari; pp 12(t), 17(t), 72-5, 186-7 © Paul Warchol; pp 12(b), 70-1 courtesy Claudio Silvestrin, © James Morris; pp 13, 15(t), 20-1, 36-40 © Christian Richters; pp 14(tl,tr+c), 24-35 © Office for Metropolitan Archtecture; pp 14(b), 42-7 © Renzo Piano Building Workshop, photos: Denancé Michel; pp 15(c), 116-21 © Alexander McQueen, photos: Eric Langel; pp 16(t), 192 courtesy of Future Systems; pp 16(b), 188-9, 194(t+bl), 195 © Future Systems, photos: Soren Aagaard; pp 17(b), 130-1, 148-55 photos: © Ramon Prat; p 18(t) © Austin Reed, photo: Adrian Wilson; pp 18(b), 184-5 © Gianfranco Ferré, photos: Paola De Pietri; p 19(t) © Jimmy Choo Ltd, photo: Jane Hanrahan; pp 19(b), 194(br) courtesy Selfridges @ PA Picselect; pp 48-51 © Jimmy Cohrssen/Louis Vuitton; pp 52-3 © Nacasa and Partners/Louis Vuitton; p 54 © N Nakagawa/Louis Vuitton; pp 56-7 © Louis Vuitton Archives; pp 58-9 © Stéphane Muratet/Louis Vuitton; pp 64-5, 68-9 © Claudio Silvestrin Archive; pp 94-7, 105-7, 110-11 © Richard Davies; pp 98-9 © Masayuki Hyashi; pp 100-1 © Yoshiko Seino; pp 102-4 © Marni, photos: Franco Rossi; pp 108-9 © Marni, photos: Eduard Heuber; pp 112-14 © Chloe/SH Architects; p 115 © Chloe International; p 141(t) © Heatherwick Studio; p 141(b) © Longchamp Archive; p 147(b) Courtesy of Marc Newson and Sébastien Segers; pp 162-7 © Paul Smith/SH Architects; pp 168-9 © Curiosity Inc., photos: Theo Delhaste; pp 170-3 © Curiosity Inc., photos: Shinichi Sato; pp 174-9 © Woo II Kim; pp 180-3 © 6a, photos: David Grandage; p 193 © Norbert Schoerner/Skylab Media; pp 218-21 © Courtesy of Dover Street Market

Preface

The first edition of *Fashion Retail* captured an epoch in which fashion retail design took a tremendous leap forward. Some of the world's best-known designers created innovative, bespoke environments that pushed architectural design further while offering customers a type of shopping experience that was previously unimaginable. Store designs for Prada, Stella McCartney, Louis Vuitton, Marni and Armani remain in this new edition, revealing themselves to have a depth to their innovation that is allowing them to stand the test of time. This second edition also includes many of the world's most exciting retail environments, and builds upon other aspects, particularly in the realms of accessories and department stores, that have recently come to the fore.

The first edition focused almost purely on clothing retail, but it has become impossible to talk about the most successful new adventures in fashion retail without highlighting environments for accessories. Thomas Heatherwick's New York store for Longchamp, the luxury bag brand, is one of the most radical and intelligent retail concepts imaginable. Marc Newson has created a circular Parisian temple for Azzedine Alaïa's shoes, and Universal Design Studio has provided the foundation for the instantaneous stellar reputation of Catriona MacKechnie's first lingerie boutique. Here, the design company has remastered the apparent weight and texture of materials to create a transition between the harsh New York Meatpacking District and the fragility of the lingerie. Accessory specialists have learned the value of good clothing retail design and have matched it. In the last few years, it is even fair to say that they have pushed the boundaries further, which coincides with the strengthening of interest in handbags and shoes – frequently the most treasured items in a fashionista's wardrobe.

Just a few years ago it looked as if department stores were entering a new era, with bespoke newbuilds changing expectations of architectural design. Traditionally, department stores are the monoliths of fashion retail design: linear, confusing and unwieldy. Future Systems' design of the Selfridges building in Birmingham promised a brave new world, but since the first edition of *Fashion Retail* went to press, little seems to have happened to convince us that the genre can lead an architectural revolution. In fact, Marks & Spencer's attempts to invigorate the genre, by hiring John Pawson for its Lifestore concept, ended in a very rapid failure. However, this new edition shows that there have been huge advances in department store design – it has just been more subtle. Working within the constraints of established, restrictive buildings, designers have developed amazing ideas that may not have the architectural 'wow' factor of Birmingham Selfridges, but have nonetheless transformed the retail experience: perhaps this is an even greater achievement than designing from scratch. Jordan Mozer's redesign of Karstadt, Universal's redefinition of Lotte in Seoul and Plajer & Franz's sympathetic interior reworking of Jean Nouvel's Galeries Lafayette in Berlin have each pushed new boundaries. Behind the designs there is a realisation that large store branding and the benefits of boutique-style shopping can coexist to foster a unique retail experience. Department stores are finally biting back against the boutiques.

In addition, the power of the Internet has become all the more pervasive. In terms of fashion retail, the most important factor has not been the continuing increase in the numbers of regular Internet users, but the rapidly increasing conversion rate from regular user to Internet shopper. There are frequent reports indicating that this online confidence is catastrophic in terms of high-street sales. However, high fashion retail is more immune to this change in shopping behaviour than cheaper, mass-market goods: when people are investing in luxury goods, by comparison with a loaf of bread or mass-market underwear, they are more likely to want a close personal and tactile relationship with the items before they buy. The price tag carries with it the concept of the bespoke, or at least of the rare and individual, and a one-dimensional experience remains flat even when web designers resort to the use of catwalk film clips and animated gifs. Furthermore, boutique shopping has the associations of a pleasurable and often shared event in a way that supermarket or general store shopping does not. As the retail projects in this new edition show, canny designers are playing up the heightened experience of a real-time, unique environment in order to offer something that a website cannot. There is an 'event dynamic' and a great reliance on texture at the heart of the most successful recent store designs.

After the turn of the century, it seemed that maximalism – a textural and design overload – was about to play a major part in building up the possibilities of the store environment. However, maximalism has never quite taken hold, but has been happily watered down to the inclusion of surprising objects that create juxtaposition, rather than a sensory overload. Particularly in Japan, it is now commonplace to see Baroque features and outlandish chandeliers set against conventional minimalist backdrops. In the UK, new stores such as PPQ Mayfair rely on the same trick, in this case merging a conventional boutique style with touches of op art and Victorian psychedelia – the jewellery case is a glass Victorian cabinet featuring malevolent-looking stuffed magpies. However, rather than relying on a juxtaposition that can sometimes seem quite forced and superficial, the most successful recent store designs push in the direction of an almost sculptural centrepiece – the focal point of an intelligent, suggestive narrative – to create the sense of 'event'.

Of all the projects included in this book, Galaxie Lafayette, set within Galeries Lafayette in Berlin, may have had the most to fear from the increase in online shopping – it is a new department specialising in young women's jeanswear – so perhaps this influenced the scale of the event the designers created. The design possibilities were constrained by the famous building's original form, but Plajer & Franz Studio has managed to create a central vortical showpiece around the tip of one of Jean Nouvel's floor-piercing glass cones. The combination of a design focusing on circular motion, live DJ music and coloured LED lighting conjures an exciting environment even for the most prematurely world-weary chatroom princess. The designers have imbued the entire floor with a spatial narrative of retro-futurism and circular motion that tells a story leading to this central event. In the years since the roster of high-design, high-fashion boutiques were paraded on the world stage around the turn of the century, mid-market labels have raised the stakes. Prada SoHo and the like have shown the benefit of good, experiential design and how it can imbue customers with a sense of uniqueness to match their aspirations. Nike has pushed forward the Niketown concept and gone ever further towards the high-fashion retail experience by creating the Nike iD Studio, a beautiful, invite-only, customised shopping experience designed by Christian Lynch and Simon Eisenger. Berlin-based Plajer & Franz is as responsible as anyone else for ratchetting up expectations of mid-market retail design by investing the likes of the German s.Oliver chain, and even Timberland, with high-design concepts.

As with Galaxie Lafayette, the designers of Azzedine Alaïa, Lotte, Catriona MacKechnie and Dover Street Market have all threaded their work with narrative, experiential and sculptural design that promises some sense of event. At Alaïa, Marc Newson has combined the concept of an oversized jewellery box with that of a shrine, with the shoes as the glittering jewels to be worshipped. At both Lotte and Catriona MacKechnie, Universal Design Studio plays with texture and pattern, controlling our focus with surprising screens and partitions, while Dover Street Market is a parade of unfolding chapters that toy with expectations. However, the establishment of a sense of event can be no greater than in Thomas Heatherwick's design for Longchamp. Faced with the problem of drawing people to an above-ground retail space, he created an alluring rolling staircase of metal ribbons which he describes as a landscape, but which could easily be termed an artwork.

Below: s.Oliver by Plajer & Franz Studio, Munich. The Munich s.Oliver branch builds on the high-design concepts that originated in fashion retail outlets to raise the image of a mid-market brand

Left and below: **Hussein Chalayan by Block Architecture, Tokyo.** Turkish Cypriot Hussein Chalayan is famous for creating almost architectural, sculptural clothing. Block Architecture was faced with the challenge of designing his Tokyo boutique, where they chose to play with people's expectations, merging a Cypriot garden with Japanese elements, and a regimented structure with apparently casual displays

Left and above: **Hairywood by 6a Architects, London.** Architects 6a worked with fashion designer Eley Kishimoto to traverse architecture, design and art in a 2005 temporary summerhouse for the Architecture Foundation. Kishimoto's pattern designs are incorporated within the structure

Heatherwick's design may be the most obvious meeting point of fashion, architectural design and art, but the genres are becoming increasingly merged in a variety of ways. Hussein Chalayan is an example of a clothing designer whose work verges on both the architectural and sculptural – he uses surprising firm materials and once developed a range that was part clothing, part furniture. Architectural designers 6a are included within this book for their radical design of the Oki-ni store. Since then they have blended art and fashion through a series of installations that unite architectural and fashion design principals to create unique environments, and have even become involved in catwalk design. Meanwhile, Dover Street Market is dedicated to being an environment where the distinctions between fashion, art and retail blur.

One of the far-reaching consequences of the rise in fashion retail design cannot be properly contained within the following pages: it deserves longer exposition. Working with some of the world's greatest designers to create such adventurous retail interiors has led a plethora of brands to use architecture and design to enable them to cross genres. Perhaps the most aesthetically successful is Bulgari's venture into the world of hotels with a design by Antonio Citterio that exemplifies the restrained quality of the famous jewellers while not comprising the validity of its architectural concept. The worlds of fashion design and hotel culture are mixed together in Azzedine Alaïa's showroom and workshop complex in Paris, where he has incorporated a three-room boutique hotel, while the Lotte department store featured in this book is connected to a Lotte hotel. Even mid-market brands such as Camper and Miss Sixty have moved into the hotel market in the belief that there is an aspirational synthesis between fashion and architectural design. Armani, though, seems to have the grandest plans, beginning a worldwide network of hotels and resorts with the Dubai Armani Hotel in 2008. Fashion and architectural design are to be closely entwined for evermore.

Howard Watson

Above and right: **Bulgari Hotel by Antonio Citterio, Milan.** Architect and designer Antonio Citterio has designed Bulgari's beautiful and serene first hotel, part of a growing trend for fashion and accessory brands to cross genres into the hotel market

Fashion and architecture

In recent years, the interests of fashion and architecture have started to truly converge. This has happened as fashion houses have begun to realise the advantage of creating strong architecturally designed spaces while architects have reaped the benefits of the employment and exposure that fashion retail can bring. One defining moment, in terms of press coverage, is the collaboration between Miuccia Prada and Rem Koolhaas in 2000, which brought the respective figureheads of the two design disciplines together in an internationally publicised architectural rebranding and rethinking of the Prada label. This, however, was a focus for an already turning tide. Whereas, previously, the

Introduction

relationship between architecture and fashion had often been ambivalent or even grudging – serving the other strictly in terms of function and display – it had already started to shift into an exciting dynamic, where one informs the other.

In the late 1980s, London saw the pared down high-tech of Eva Jiricna's designs for Joseph on Sloane Street and the 'shop as shrine' minimalism of David Chipperfield for Issey Miyake as clear demonstrations of a new synergy with fashion. The stripped-down architectural styles created a perfect backdrop for the black and white tailoring of the 1980s and early 1990s. Now, some 20 years later, it's possible to see fashion and architecture in terms of what they share and how they might be benefiting from collaboration. Both are about all things new; both are about responding to history with a creative form and about making manifest cultural ideas; and both are about the discovery of new materials and technologies. In addition, fashion benefits as architecture creates a platform upon which it can be displayed, and architects are able to realise their work in physical form faster than with any other building type – often in little more than three months.

Architecture and fashion first discovered their reciprocal link within the context of the department store. Here was the first instance where the

Jil Sander by Michael Gabellini, London.
Michael Gabellini has been designing minimalist and elegant stores for Jil Sander since 1993 and has completed 31 stores for the brand worldwide

Prada by Herzog & de Meuron, Tokyo.
The architects created the whole building as a display window for Prada

marketplace found architectural form bringing many brands, rather than stores, under one roof. For the first time, interior display became the critical factor that would encourage the sale of one particular brand over another. This was the key to the relationship: architecture and fashion can gain from an understanding of each other's approach to design.

Outside the department store, the possibilities for architects in fashion retail were regarded as limited. In terms of a hierarchy of building types, retail or shop refits were the bottom of the heap. They were the starting point for an architectural career rather than the pinnacle. The phenomenon of signature architects of the stature of Frank Gehry being attracted to work for fashion houses was unknown. It was not until the late 1980s and early 1990s that there was a discernible shift in the way that architects started to view fashion retail work. This was prompted by a recession that hit larger architectural schemes hard, but left an opening in retail with the steady rise in consumer spending. Perhaps the most prominent late 1980s examples of this were Branson Coates's 'aeroplane facade' for Jigsaw on Knightsbridge and the Katharine Hamnett store on Sloane Street, with a fishtank prominently placed in the window. However, the idea of architecture and fashion teaming up to inform the brand was not on the agenda of the time, and instead these sometimes 'baroque' and flamboyant interiors (in the case of Branson Coates) remained distinct and unique alongside the first minimalist boutiques coming through from David Chipperfield and John Pawson.

As minimalism emerged as the dominant style in the 1990s, it nurtured new understandings and allegiances between fashion designers and architects. Fashion designers, whose work is predominantly clean-cut and spare, aligned themselves with architects whose work is of that nature. For example, minimalist design guru Pawson was invited to create the store concept for minimalist fashion guru Calvin Klein, and clean-cut fashion designer Giorgio Armani teamed up with the clean-cut architect Claudio Silvestrin. Other pared down fashion/architect teams include Michael Gabellini for Jil Sander and Peter Marino for Donna Karan. The minimalist store acts as a beautifully crafted empty shell for the display of beautifully crafted objects. No expense is spared on materials that are often the most luxurious of the interior palette. In some ways, this emptiness could be said to be the perfect environment for garments and their accessories to be viewed, admired and purchased. For all its merits, minimalism is a style that suits most, but not all.

The new millennium

As fashion gleaned the rewards of being associated with such named architects, as the minimalists demonstrated, fashion houses and individual clothes designers have, in recent years, generated a whole new breed of store. They

Giorgio Armani by Claudio Silvestrin, London.
Claudio Silvestrin has now designed over 27 stores worldwide for Giorgio Armani, complementing the sleek lines of the garments with his monastic-like minimalism using only the most exquisite materials

Prada by Rem Koolhaas,
SoHo, New York.

Prada by Rem Koolhaas, SoHo, New York.
This Prada store in New York, designed by
Rem Koolhaas was commissioned to the tune
of $40 million

Prada by Rem Koolhaas, SoHo, New York.
Beyond restructuring the physical reality of the
brand in three realised projects in the US, Koolhaas
and OMA have designed extensive in-store
technology projects that have generated a new
integrated service structure for Prada, and aim to
give Prada (the brand) the edge on exclusivity

have chosen signature architects, and through the assimilation of the brand into the architecture (whether by the architects' intent or by the intense relationship between architect and fashion designer), a new element of the brand has been brought to life: the store now embodies the concepts of the brand. Never before have Pritzker Prize level architects such as Herzog & de Meuron, Rem Koolhaas and Renzo Piano been associated with fashion. Now, such names are leading the shoppers into the new 'shopping temples' of our consumer culture.

It has been a very exciting time for both fashion houses and architects, as architecture finds a new forum of expression in the world of retail, and fashion designers find their styles extended into the store. Working in fashion is incredibly free and creative, according to many architects, as it allows them to design environments that play on the relationship between outside and inside, and to design spaces that can respond to the transitions from season to season. In addition, designing for spaces that typically have a relatively short shelf life gives the project a certain cutting edge – the design has to have an immediate impact to make its mark if it is only going to be around for, at best, five years.

Projects range from interior refits to entire buildings, and the budgets reflect such diversity. The buildings may be monumental in scale and are incredible in both concept and form. Fashion, it could be argued, is the new forum for exciting architecture, and its potential is enormous (which is sometimes overlooked due to its association with an often 'whimsical' industry). Fashion houses are allowing, and even encouraging, architects to explore spaces, to push boundaries, to experiment with technologies and to present an ever-responding environment within which to display their products.

An act of distinction

The context of these commissions is one of design overload: we are bombarded with design in our everyday lives and brand names struggle to keep afloat amongst this sea of competition. Architecture is part of distinguishing the fashion brand from so many rivals and imitators. Architecture must create the narrative that grabs the customers' attention and lures them into the world of the brand.

To take one well-known brand, Prada: the label is designed to become a whole way of life, a way of being, and it is the environment within which Prada is placed that carries these messages. As Aaron Betsky points out, 'The importance of such environments was succinctly shown by the artist Andreas Gursky when he photographed Prada's familiar (to some) lime-green shoe display case without a single shoe in it. Not the product, but the scene is the point.'[1] It is interesting to note Betsky's own brackets and assumption that such a scene is already familiar to a Prada-aware audience.

Fashion's architectural commissions are also within a context of a very real

Hermès by Renzo Piano, Tokyo.

Prada by Herzog & de Meuron, Tokyo.
The Tokyo store by Herzog & de Meuron cost Prada $87 million

Alexander McQueen by Will Russell, New York.
Alexander McQueen stores, now part of the Gucci group, are designed by young London architect Will Russell

Stella McCartney by
Universal Design Studio, London.
Stella McCartney is one of the younger brands belonging to Gucci. This is reflected in the innovative and modern decorative approach of London-based Universal Design Studios stores

and fluctuating world economy, where survival of the fittest seems to be the underlying theme. These economic factors and the need for brand differentiation have had considerable impact on the brand's policies, and are not to be overlooked in determining the relationship between fashion and architecture.

Fashion and figures

The fashion industry is as vulnerable to economic swings as any other industry. Recently, the war in Iraq, the SARS epidemic and the euro's strength against the dollar have all been reflected in the reported losses of the big fashion names. This slump is also in the context of a slow recession that we have endured for some years since the dot.com bubble burst in the late 1990s.

Much to our surprise, however, but in keeping with tradition, perhaps super-luxury purchases have not been so negatively affected as predicted. The extremely wealthy have continued to shop for the top of the range luxury items without too much hesitation: the latest BMW sports cars, Cartier gems, Chanel dresses and named luxury fur coats have all continued to sell well.

In reaction to this slump, however, some of the big fashion names have carried themselves over to the mass market, moving away from the exclusive, elitist customer that they traditionally sought. They have been working on attracting the 'mass-affluent' market. Prada handbags, Gucci sunglasses and Louis Vuitton suitcases have now become familiar items amongst the new middle-class buyers.

Dilution

This mass-marketing which became very evident amongst the top brands towards the end of the 1990s – a trend that reflected the 'show-off' attitudes of the prior economic period – pushed the label to reach its peak in terms of popularity. The brand name really found itself 'out there' amongst the masses. This popularity in turn knocked the edge off its 'exclusiveness', as the brand was paraded *en masse*. Luxury goods had found their mass market and their logos were placed everywhere, whether original or fake. In essence, the brand became diluted and lost its strength.

At the same time, the bosses of the big fashion houses acquired handfuls of the luxury brands, uniting them under one holding company – in turn offering financial discipline and good commercial practice. The top end of the fashion industry is now dominated by three groups: Louis Vuitton Moët Hennessy (LVMH), Prada and Gucci.

Whilst allowing the brand to flourish in popularity, consolidation, like mass appeal, also weakened the brand and challenged the notion of 'exclusivity'. Once the brand has lost some of its credibility the fashion house seeks to re-establish value and attract custom. Making bold investments at this point in the brand's shelf life can be seen to be very high risk, indeed immodest, but this approach seems to be the model for the way forward in order to bring the elitist, high-quality status back to the name.

Bold investments, bold design, brand differentiation

These bold investments often come in the form of financing new architecture. In the last five years 'signature' architects have been invited to bring their creative vision to literally 'house' the brand, and we are seeing some incredibly strong, sometimes beautiful and definitely innovative results. Architecture – exterior and interior – is being used to bring a certain social cachet back to the brand name.

By association with top-name architects, fashion houses are adding weight to their name, conferring an almost serious, disciplined edge to a sometimes ill-disciplined industry that is typically associated with flamboyant and dramatic

1 Aaron Betsky, 'A Matching for Living', *Logique/Visuelle: The Architecture of Louis Vuitton 2003*, Louis Vuitton (Japan (2003)

personalities. The amounts being spent today on the architecture behind the brand are astounding – budgets that would have been assigned to museums and monuments a decade ago.

For example, Prada brought on board the outspoken architect Rem Koolhaas in 2001 for its store in New York at a cost of $40 million, and Herzog de Meuron, the famed Swiss architects of the Tate Modern in London, for their recent store in Tokyo to the tune of $87 million.

Before Tom Ford's acrimonious split with Gucci in 2004, he chose New York's cool Bill Sofield to give a fresh, light look for the group's YSL stores – the brand which the Gucci group are currently revamping. In addition, Alexander McQueen and Stella McCartney, also part of the Gucci group, have commissioned known architects and interior designers – Will Russell and Universal Design Studio – to strengthen their identity. However, it remains to be seen whether Pinault Printemps Redoute, Gucci's new owner, will allow the consequent level of expenditure to continue.

Even our homegrown department store – Selfridges – has boldly put itself on Birmingham's map, dominating the cityscape with its futuristic blue and silver facade. Designed by Future Systems, who have an established name in the retail world, this curvaceous building was inspired by a Paco Rabanne dress and wraps around the corner of the Bullring shopping centre like a piece of sequined fabric. The building is already being used as a city landmark in regional media.

Departures or extensions

Another trend that is emerging in response to the competition amongst fashion brands to keep one step ahead of each other, is the expansion into other market sectors. More and more fashion houses are now offering extensive homeware selections in amongst their clothing collections. For example, Nicole Farhi has been designing her own range of interiors for some time and, indeed, some of her more recent stores are incorporating display units for such items. Ralph Lauren has just recently launched a whole new chain of stores dedicated to homeware, aptly named Ralph Lauren Home. Similarly, the Armani group have established the Armani Casa stores (translated as Armani Home).

Others also offer significant spaces for eateries: Nicole Farhi's New York store is now more or less equally divided between fashion collections and a restaurant, and the Emporio Armani chain now offers cafés, restaurants, beauty salons and bookshops. Even the new Austin Reed flagship store in London's Regent Street has an entire floor dedicated to men's grooming. But top of the list of add-ons to stores has to be the Gianfranco Ferré Boutique and Spa in Milan. This historic palazzo is now home to all things luxurious, including a wonderful Zen-like spa.

It is interesting also to see the wonderfully designed stores for Jimmy Choo that have recently opened in New York, Milan and London, which reveal the renowned shoe designer's investment in interior architecture as a way to enhance the stores' designs and promote the brand.

Frocks, shoes, handbags, cushions, bedspreads and more, the fashion houses seem not only to be responding to increasing competition by differentiating themselves still further, but also by buying into the concept of 'lifestyle' as something that can be developed, marketed and sold. In addition, each brand now has its own 'fashion sunglasses', 'fashion perfumes', 'fashion watches' etc. that are all part of the 'lifestyle' thing. Customers are buying into the brand at all levels in an all-pervading, almost invasive way, like never before.

Store as stage

Stores are also diversifying by offering themselves as venues for art or other cultural events. Rem Koolhaas's design for Prada SoHo, New York includes a platform that emerges on command from the wavelike stairs to host cultural or

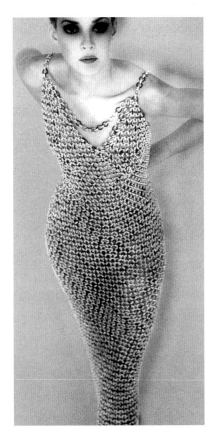

Selfridges by Future Systems, Birmingham.
The Paco Rabanne dress inspired Future Systems' concept for the new Selfridges department store in Birmingham, 2003

Selfridges by Future Systems, Birmingham.
This store now acts as the city's architectural landmark

Nicole Farhi by Michael Gabellini, New York.
As well as selling homeware, one third of the store is dedicated to a restaurant

music events, the display steps offering themselves as an auditorium for the audience. In London, Will Russell's designs for Margaret Howell stores (not included here), in contrast to his designs for Alexander McQueen, create a gallery out of the store, blurring the division between shop and gallery, and between garments and art objects. Virgile and Stone's designs for Burberry in Milan include a variety of art pieces and installations by a wide range of artists.

Pushing the idea right to its edge has to be Selfridges' recent 'Body Craze' event at their famous Oxford Street store. Staged in early 2003, 'Body Craze' was an art exhibition, termed an 'uninhibited celebration of the human form', in which 500 naked people struck a pose on its escalators as artist Spencer Tunick and press photographers recorded the scene. Has Selfridges set itself up as a 'retail theme park', as one critic put it, staging events to encourage shoppers? It seems that its mad methods have worked, as recent figures show an increase in sales and trading profits.

Democratising luxury: profile of the new shopper[2]

In keeping with the new extensions to the brand is a new type of luxury goods' consumer who is seen as a key to market expansion. These new consumers are 'democratising luxury', according to one economist. They are middle-market consumers aspiring to higher levels of quality and taste who are carrying luxury goods into another social stratum.

As we see on the high street and at airports, people are wearing a $10 T-shirt by H&M or Gap and carrying a $500 bag by Gucci, or wearing a $300 watch by Calvin Klein and enjoying the aromas of the new Stella McCartney perfume at $50 a bottle. These new consumers show less brand loyalty, and are more selective than the consumers of traditional luxury products such as Cartier, YSL or Dior. They are also younger than their traditional counterparts and want the latest designs off the press.

Emporio Armani by Fuksas & Fuksas, Hong Kong.
The store includes a restaurant, flowershop, bookshop, café and beauty salon

2 'Every cloud has a satin lining', *The Economist*, 21 March 2003

However, as mentioned earlier, if the goods become too popular they lose their value, and a brand name can easily become undermined if displayed incorrectly, or advertised poorly. For example, in response to the dilution of its name, Gucci has been buying back its brand licensing to ensure its logo only appears on products which meet its own standards of quality. The 'execution' of the luxury goods business is critical to its success or failure and in this case, the execution is about retailing. Today, 80 per cent of Gucci's and Hermès' products, and all of Louis Vuitton's, are sold through directly owned or operated stores.

In addition, shoppers now have the option to shop from home via the designers' websites, including cut-price brand products. In order to compete with the new electronic retailing, the store needs to offer a memorable and worthwhile environment for the brand, making the experience of shopping much more desirable than simply 'point and click'.

Architecture and its social cachet

Returning to the original assumption that the association between architecture and fashion can bring added value to the fashion house, the question that needs examination is how a building really can give social cachet to the products it houses. Can the interior spaces and hanging rails really inform the customer about the brand?

The store is where the sale takes place and as with any other business model, it is in the execution of the business that you have to get the equation right. For fashion, this is the point of sale which means placing the right product in the right environment at the right time.

The surrounding built environment can inform the customer about the brand by reinforcing its identity with style. For example, fashion designers that are renowned for sleek lines and simple cuts tend to use architects who will reflect this in built form, and those better known for more flamboyant and colourful tailoring will tend to commission architects who will complement this style.

Today, in our all-consuming, all-pervading culture, when we purchase a product we are buying into the brand. The building, the logo, the advertising, the fashion model, even the shop assistants, in addition to the clothes and accessories themselves, all tie up this thing called 'image' or brand. In a sense, buying into this is like buying into a club membership. A customer will identify with a brand that reflects his or her tastes and will gravitate towards those names, reinforcing his or her self-image, just as one becomes a member of a club. One of the qualities that architecture can give to the overall image bought into by the customer, is in the all-encompassing nature of the built form: the store is more than just products and may say something about a way of doing, a way

Austin Reed, London.
The new flagship offers an entire floor dedicated to men's grooming

Gianfranco Ferré Boutique, Milan.
The store offers shop and spa all in one, both bathed in absolute luxury

Jimmy Choo, London.
The shoe chain is also taking note of the importance of interior architecture as its brand new store that opened in December 2003 on Bond Street shows. 'Sex in the City' has helped create a huge middle market for fashion house accessories such as Manolo Blahnik shoes and Prada handbags. In order to preserve their share of the market, specialist designers such as Jimmy Choo have to make sure that their retail outlets can compete at the highest level

of being, or a way to organise your own home. The design of a space can represent our social background, our income, our cultural values, our age, our aspirations. Architecture can put cities back on the map – as Frank Gehry did with the Guggenheim Museum in Bilbao or as Future Systems have recently done in Birmingham with the new Selfridges store. Architecture then, is able to give the brand its social cachet once again, and help the brand to become one of the most talked about names of the decade, without the risk of brand dilution.

Fashion and its benefits

What then for the architect? Apart from publicity on the fashion pages (which can be very powerful and effective), how can working in the fashion industry inform or promote the architect?

Could we ever consume a building or its interiors in the same way we consume a beautiful piece of clothing? Of course not. We can't acquire the building, the room, the staircase, the changing rooms, the display case, or the wardrobes, we can't take them to the cash desk to be wrapped in tissue paper for us to take home.

Or maybe we could. Taking this idea to its extreme – maybe by shopping in one of these stores we will also be informed about the architecture and the design, and we will be able to buy objects by the architect, or have the architect design for our own homes. Already it is not unusual to hear that a shop's architect also designed the home of a fashion icon, or to read about the long-term loyalty between architect and fashion designer such as Gabellini and Jil Sander or Claudio Silvestrin and Giorgio Armani. Wherever it is heading, the association between fashion and architecture is yielding some positive economic and cultural results for both sides.

The case studies in this book are presented in four chapters. The first chapter, Spectacular Houses, looks at the incredible architectural and interior projects commissioned by the larger fashion houses including Louis Vuitton, Prada and Hermès. The second chapter, Architectural Branding, takes as its theme the synergy between architect and fashion designer as emergent in the interior architecture developed for the brand worldwide. What is interesting here is how clearly the architect's style of work relates directly to the style of the brand he is designing for. The third chapter, Custom Made, looks at commissions by fashion houses that result in a one-off store, which although very much in line with the fashion designer's brand is also led by the location of the store. Even if an architect works on several commissions for the same fashion house, the result may not be a 'branding' of the architecture.

The final chapter, New Departments, presents case studies where new and innovative architectural design is being commissioned for the larger store. Although markedly different in style, content and philosophy, as well as size, to the other fashion houses in this book, these projects demonstrate how important interiors and architecture are becoming as the new forum upon which to distinguish and present the brand within a massive department store. They also show how department stores can use design to offer a multilayered experience for ever more discerning customers.

'Body Craze' in Selfridges, London.
Like Prada SoHo, Selfridges London now has a direct relationship with culture, encouraging an idea of the brand beyond the normal function of retail. A groundbreaking involvement with the Japan 2000 Festival was followed by this 'art exhibition' of 600 naked people riding up and down the store's escalators

Spectacular Houses

In the realm of fashion and architecture, one of the most remarkable things the public have witnessed in the last few years is the construction of a number of impressive buildings, monumental in scale, for the big fashion houses. Two of the three dominant fashion conglomerates – Louis Vuitton and Prada – are not only leaders in terms of luxury and fashion, but are also important 'patrons' to architecture, leading architects to push design to the edge in terms of how it can serve fashion. The buildings are innovative, creative and high-tech, and interestingly, the allocated budgets are equivalent in value to those spent on public museums and other important institutions 10–15 years ago.

The whole notion of commissioning new buildings to house fashion is an interesting idea that says a lot about the importance of fashion and consumerism, or consumer behaviour. In one sense, the fashion house is attempting to promote or preserve the idea of 'exclusivity', in that the goods that it sells under a particular brand name are available only to a select few, and in turn the brand name has come to signify an exclusive range of products with a certain set of standards. Indeed, commissioning a new

Spectacular Houses

building may serve to reinforce this sense of the brand and the exclusiveness of the environment within which it is housed.

At the same time, however, the fashion house needs to be 'inclusive' or open to a wider public in order to increase its sales and to push its name even further into the public realm. Architecture can enable this in its design and its association: the 'look' of the building can promote a sense of openness and invitation, whilst an association with a signature architect, or even just the discipline of architecture, can widen the scope of the fashion brand.

In addition, there is the consumer response: astonishingly enough, the night before many of these newly commissioned buildings opened, long queues would start to form down the street. Brand loyalists inconvenienced themselves to sleep overnight on the street in order to be the first to experience the new architecture. (Examples include the opening of the Roppongi store by Louis Vuitton in Japan, and the Prada store by Herzog & de Meuron in Tokyo, both 2003.)

Presented in this chapter are some recent architectural designs for buildings, facades and interiors for the larger named brands. The majority of projects are in Asia, due mostly to the availability of land and the more relaxed regulations for construction.

Two of the projects are by established European architects for European brands in Tokyo and New York. Renzo Piano, the Italian architect perhaps most widely known for his design for the Pompidou Art Centre in Paris (1977, with UK architect Richard Rogers), designed the new headquarters for Hermès in Tokyo in the form of a 'magic lantern'; a tall, thin and elegant 11-storey building housing all things 'Hermès' from retail through to exhibition space. Dutch architect Rem Koolhaas's designs for Prada in New York, though largely interior architecture, result in the most innovative commentary on shopping and brands to date. New technologies are integrated in the store in a way that transforms the ritual of shopping into something more than just the purchase, subsuming the clients into the brand they are investing in. Ironic, then, that Koolhaas made his name in the mid-1990s with his infamous text *S, M, L, XL* that entailed a critique on architecture and consumerism.

The other projects are for Louis Vuitton stores, worldwide, that are not only outstanding in their brand-inspired designs, but also in that Louis Vuitton has gathered its own in-house architectural team to realise this physical extension of the luxury brand. The Paris-based team, led by David McNulty and Eric Carlson, works on an incredible 50–100 stores per year that can entail anything from an entire building or a facade to an interior refit. The team also works with other architectural studios who are invited to supply concepts for new stores, overseen by the Louis Vuitton in-house team. A number of projects are presented here offering a range of works – from new buildings and facades in Japan and Korea to earlier ideas for interior refits in Paris and New York. Most notable are the designs for the Roppongi store in Japan, which takes on the theme of a nightclub, and the Omotesando store whose facade is shaped like a random stack of Louis Vuitton trunks. In no other project is the translation of brand icon into architectural form as apparent.

Rem Koolhaas and the
Office for Metropolitan Architecture

Prada Epicentre

SoHo, New York 2001

Rem Koolhass and his Office for Metropolitan Architecture were invited by Prada to develop three themes in fashion retail: the design of new retail concepts for the brand; the creation of three big stores in the US; and to broadly contribute to new ideas about shopping. Although criticised in some quarters, the results have certainly marked a new departure for fashion retail.

The Dutch architect Rem Koolhaas is perhaps better known for his critiques on architecture and consumerism, including *S, M, L, XL* (010 Publications, 1995) and *The Harvard Guide to Shopping* (Taschen, 2001), than for his buildings. Prada, in turn, is known for its distinct lines of high fashion and its director, Miuccia Prada, for her very strong views on art, architecture and shopping. It was of great interest to both architects and cultural theorists alike that Prada should ask the controversial critic of consumerism to come up with some new ideas for shopping, in built form. Gossipmongers also had a field day as there were rumours of an affair between Prada and Koolhaas.

Beyond restructuring the physical reality of the brand in three realised projects in the US, Koolhaas and OMA have designed extensive in-store technology projects that have generated a new integrated service structure for Prada and aims to give the brand the edge on exclusivity.

Instead of a traditional flagship store, Prada conceived an 'epicentre' which would offer a diversified experience of shopping. The epicentre store is divided into many zones: the clinic, an environment for personal care and service; the archive, an inventory of current and past collections; the trading floor, an accumulation of rapidly changing information, new technologies and e-commerce; the library, areas of content and knowledge of fashion; and the street, a space for multiple activities, liberated from the pressure to buy.

The New York Epicentre is a conversion of the former Guggenheim store in SoHo, an area famous for its progressive art galleries and young urbanites – a world away from Prada's other, more typical high-profile site on Fifth Avenue. On entering the store, the 'wave' of stairs leads to the lower floor, connecting both levels with a vast wooden sculpture of steps. The oversized stair, made of zebra wood, is also an informal

Above and below: **Prada Epicentre New York.**
The grand staircase, or wave, is made of zebra wood and also acts as an informal display space. The adjacent translucent polycarbonate creates a dialogue between old and new as it slightly reveals the original brick wall

Above: **Prada Epicentre New York.** Site plan

Above: **Prada Epicentre New York.** The lower level can be seen through the shaft of the cylindrical glass elevator. The 12 foot diameter 'cab' contains a display of bags, so clients can shop on their way down to the lower floor

display space for shoes and mannequins. Encased in the stair is an event platform that emerges at the push of a button, turning the area into a 200-seat auditorium for cultural events organised by the Prada Foundation. This transition is at the heart of Prada and Koolhaas's vision to transform a retail space into a venue for art-happenings in New York's cool SoHo.

Large metal cages used as display units are suspended overhead on a track system like a 'hanging city'. Even the elevator is used to display bags and other accessories. A translucent, polycarbonate wall covers the existing brick of the building, lining the stairs, and creating a dialogue between old and new.

The main lounge under the wave is also where the main dressing rooms are located. Visible from display 'mattresses' covered in techno-gel, the transparency of the room may be controlled from within the dressing room itself, so a viewer may watch someone get dressed. The dressing rooms also feature other high-tech installations: 'magic mirrors' allow the customer to see themselves from both front and back at the same time, and an integrated time-delay function can even capture and replay moments. Equipped with Radio Frequency Identity antennae, the 'garment closet' is able to register merchandise brought into the room and subsequently display an inventory of icons on a touch screen. The customer can then request additional information or browse through alternative collections.

It has been reported that these technological advances are beset with functional problems, and when they are working, they are more a curiosity for tourists than an in-store aid for Prada shoppers. There are other issues, too, including negative remarks about the quality of the detailing and the unethical use of zebra wood. Perhaps this new approach to retail has been compromised too much for the sake of 'art' and 'design', and the space resembles more a museum than a store, carrying with it the semi-sterile message of 'look but don't touch'. It seems that some Prada shoppers prefer to spend their dollars at the Fifth Avenue branch while SoHo is filled with non-purchasing tourists looking at the architecture. Despite the use of the auditorium for selected art events (such as the Tribeca Film Festival 2003), the space hase not been used for more radical art events as was envisioned. To some, it seems that a reportedly financially troubled fashion house has spent $40 million on a free tourist attraction.

The other two US epicentre stores by Rem Koolhaas and OMA are located in Los Angeles and San Francisco. A fourth epicentre for Prada, designed by Swiss architects Herzog & de Meuron, opened in Tokyo in 2003.

Left and above: **Prada Epicentre New York.**
Merchandise is displayed in movable volumes consisting of a number of aluminium-mesh cages. Suspended from the ceiling, they are configured to include hanging bars, shelving and space for mannequins and other displays. The units are mounted on motorised tracks so they can be positioned differently throughout the store

Below: **Prada Epicentre New York.**
Diagonal section through the hidden stage in the stairs

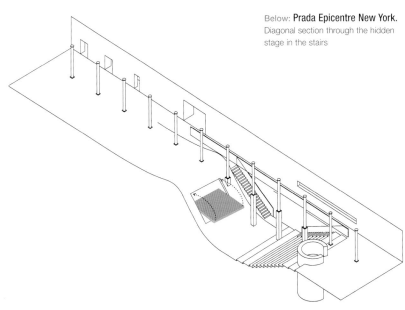

Above: Prada Epicentre New York. Suspended metal cages display Prada bags and shoes

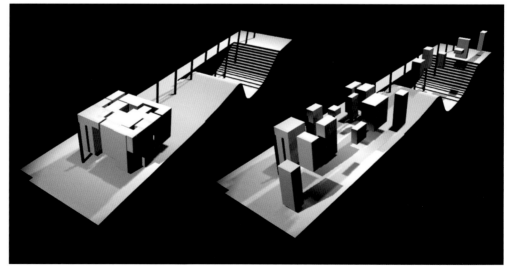

Right: Prada Epicentre New York. Computerised model of 'hanging city', with both open and clustered displays

Above: **Prada Epicentre New York.** Customers browse within the 'hanging city' of display units

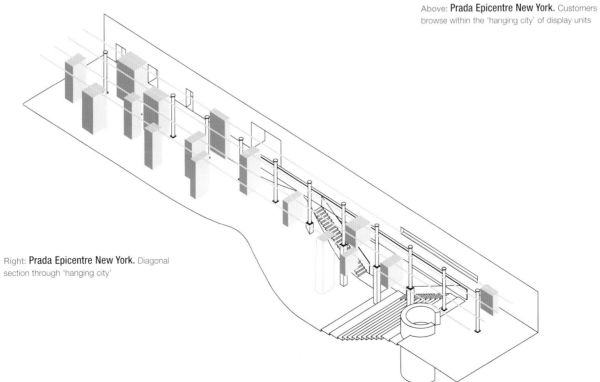

Right: **Prada Epicentre New York.** Diagonal section through 'hanging city'

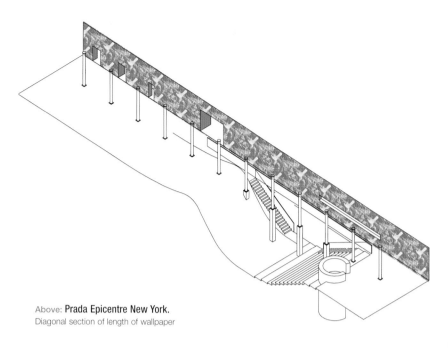

Above: **Prada Epicentre New York.**
Diagonal section of length of wallpaper

Right: **Prada Epicentre New York.**
A mural of wallpaper along the entire
length of the store offers yet another type
of environment within this retail space

Above: **Prada Epicentre New York.**
The store retains some typical SoHo
architectural details such as the raw
supporting columns on the far wall

Above: Prada Epicentre New York.
The view to the outside world is
almost unrestricted

Right: **Prada Epicentre New York.** The black and
white marble floor on the lower level makes
reference to the first Prada store in Milan;
its reflection is distorted through the curved,
mirrored ceiling of the space

Above, left and opposite: **Prada Epicentre New York.** Submerged into the display system of the store are electronic screens that show related displays of catwalks or Prada's involvement in sport or the arts, but can also be used by staff and customer as a means of communication

Herzog & de Meuron

Prada Epicentre

Tokyo 2003

Following on from Prada's ambitious projects in the USA by Rem Koolhaas, most notably in New York, Prada commissioned Swiss duo Herzog & de Meuron to design their Tokyo Epicentre store in the fashionable district of Aoyama. Famed for their designs for the Tate Modern in London and the recent award-winning Laban Dance Centre, also in London, Herzog & de Meuron have created an extraordinary building to house Prada's fashions. They have abandoned traditional notions of the storefront in favour of a tower in which display is everything and the distinction between fashion and architecture becomes blurred.

The creation of the six-storey, five-sided glass tower enabled the architects to maximise the vertical volume of the building within its permitted gross floor area. (It is hoped that the remaining part of the lot will be a plaza, similar to the public spaces of European cities.)

The shape of the building is influenced by the possible angles of view; depending on where the onlooker is standing, the body of the building may look like either a crystal or an archaic building with a saddle roof. Its glazed surface, structured as a rhomboid-shaped grid, is clad on all five sides with a combination of convex, concave and flat panels of glass, some transparent and others etched for privacy in the changing rooms. The skin of the store looks as though it is breathing, sucking in at some angles and pouting out at others. The interiors are also characterised by disappearing surfaces or elements bubbling out of the ceilings. These different geometries offer a dazzling array of reflections which give the onlooker, either inside or outside, an ever-changing view of the Prada products, the city and themselves.

The grid design of the facade is more than aesthetic: it is part of the structural engineering. Linked to the vertical cores of the building, it supports the double-height ceilings. The horizontal steel tubing helps to stiffen the overall structure and also contains private areas dedicated to the changing rooms, display units or cash desk. Multiple stairs add to the complexity of the building, which is punctuated with irregular forms intersecting the space at varying angles. 'Snorkel'-shaped multimedia displays poke around the interiors like something from a sci-fi movie, offering continual footage of Prada's international collections.

All fittings, lamps and furniture are newly designed for the store and are made of either hyper-artificial materials like silicon and fibreglass, or at the other extreme, natural textures like leather, hairy pony-skin, moss or porous planks of wood.

The tower has a 'tail': a narrow wall, with oak as its main material, curls around the edge of the site, opening onto a flight of stairs that leads to the building's basement. The tail finishes with living green moss that sprouts through small squares.

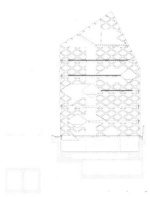

Left: Prada Tokyo. The building abandons traditional notions of storefront in favour of a five-sided tower that acts as a big display window

Right: Prada Tokyo. Sections

Below and right: Prada Tokyo. The different geometries offer a dazzling array of reflections, which give the onlooker, either inside or outside, an ever-changing view of the Prada products, the city and themselves

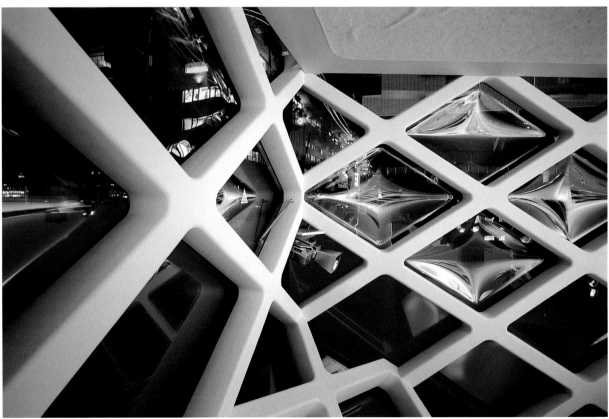

Above and left: Prada Tokyo. The double-height interior spaces are interrupted with horizontal steel tubes, that can contain changing rooms or display units. Some have 'snorkels' that house mutlimedia images of the building or of Prada's collections

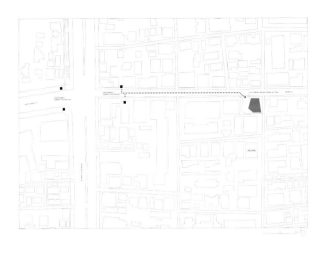

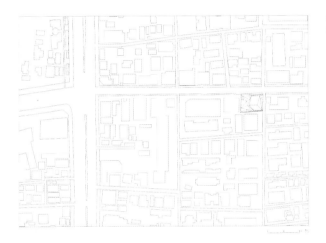

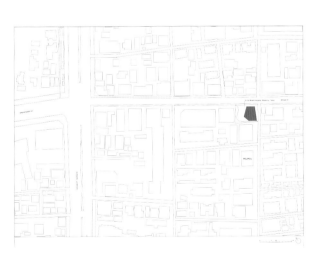

Left and right: **Prada Tokyo.**
Plans of store

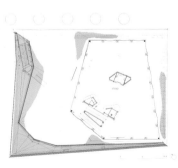

Renzo Piano Building Workshop
in collaboration with Rena Dumas
Architecture Intérieure (Paris)

Hermès

Tokyo 2001

Renzo Piano is perhaps one of today's most versatile architects. His Genoa-based office – the Renzo Piano Building Workshop – has a remarkable list of buildings and projects to its name, including landmark schemes such as the Pompidou Art Centre in Paris, Kansai Airport in Osaka, high-quality commercial buildings and a new pilgrim centre. No surprise then that Hermès invited him, with his innovative architectural vision, to design their Japanese headquarters in the Ginza district of Tokyo.

This tall, thin and elegant 11-storey building of 6,000 square metres now houses not only shopping spaces, but also floors dedicated to workshops, offices, exhibition areas and, at the top, a French-style hanging garden. With its impressive and earthquake-resistant glass-brick facade, the Maison Hermès shines like a 'magic lantern' at night.

For Piano, this project provided both aesthetic and technical challenges. How, within the architectural diversity of Tokyo, could a distinct 'landmark' building be conceived and, in turn, comply with the strict anti-seismic standards in Japan? The notion of the building lighting up Ginza like a 'magic lantern' became the dominant theme.

The dimensions of this slim building are 45 metres long and only 11 metres wide. The facades are comprised entirely of specially designed glass blocks of 45 square centimetres, creating a continuous and luminous screen between the quiet of the inner spaces and the busy city streets. This play on interior and exterior, which changes from day to night, gives a slightly technological edge to the building, whilst retaining the concept of the traditional Japanese lantern.

A small, open square at the centre of the building connects the street to the subway station from two levels below, via a long escalator integrated into the project. A mobile sculpture by Susumu Shingu was commissioned to overlook this space from the entire height of the building, playing on the light between the facade, the city and the sky.

To cater for the possibility of earthquakes, the entire building has been designed to absorb movement according to pre-defined displacements. The backbone of the building is made up of a flexible steel structure that is articulated at strategic locations with visco-elastic dampers, from which cantilevered floors span to support the suspended glass-block facades. The integrity of the building's structure is thus guaranteed, as is that of the numerous networks that comprise the building. It is also both watertight and airtight.

Above: **Hermès Tokyo.** Detailed interior view of a corner point of the glass facade made entirely of glass bricks. The building's transparent skin allows a play between interior and exterior, and the building to change its image from day to night

Right: **Hermès Tokyo.** The entrance on the ground floor at night. The area is flooded with light and a sculpture hangs overhead emphasising the verticality of the building

Left, and right top and bottom: Hermès Tokyo.
Exterior views of the building, day and night. The glass facade gives the building its slight high-tech edge, whilst at night it reflects the architect's concept of a 'magic lantern'

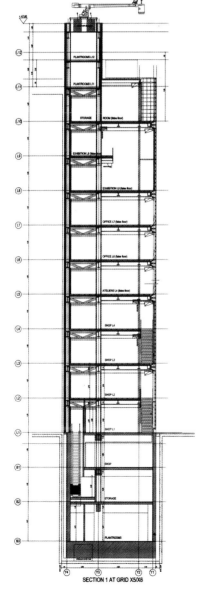

SECTION 1 AT GRID X5/X6

Left: Hermès Tokyo.
Section

Above: Hermès Tokyo. Interior of shop floor, flooded with natural light at the far end. A neutral palette has been used by interior designer Rena Dumas to complement the luxurious range of clothes, bags and scarves

Below **Hermès Tokyo.**
Plan of ground floor

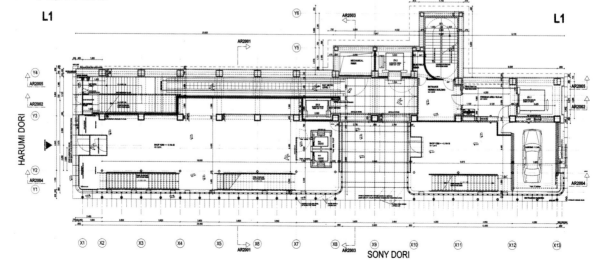

Above and right: Hermès Tokyo. The eleventh floor is given over to a French-style hanging garden while other floors are dedicated to exhibition space or multimedia installations

Louis Vuitton architects

and associated architects

Louis Vuitton stores

SoHo, New York 1998 (Louis Vuitton architects)
Nagoya 1999 (Jun Aoki & Associates)
Seoul 2000 (Eric Carlson/David McNulty)
Roppongi, Tokyo 2003 (Aurelio Clementi/Jun Aoki/Eric Carlson)
Paris 2003 (Louis Vuitton architects)
Ginza, Tokyo 2004 (Jun Aoki & Associates)

The post-1997 architectural designs for the Louis Vuitton stores worldwide are finally being acknowledged as a remarkable investment and achievement in architecture. In the Aedes East gallery in Berlin, May 2003, an exhibition of the architectural work by Louis Vuitton's Paris-based in-house architectural team and associated architectural offices was titled 'Inclusive – One brand, six architects, 11 projects'; 'Inclusive' in the sense that the architecture is part of the brand's identity and is recognised as such.

Known worldwide for its luxury bags, cases and trunks with its distinctive motifs, Louis Vuitton moved into 'fashion' in 1997 with the launch of a ready-to-wear collection. This in turn stimulated the expansion of the stores with the focus on distinctive building designs related to location. With sites mostly in Asia, the group have had the opportunity to purchase or lease land parcels on which to construct entirely new buildings dedicated to the brand. In other instances, again due to the more relaxed building regulations in Asia, the team have redesigned the entire facade of a building, giving it a new skin. In Europe and North America, where exterior changes have been minimal, interior redesign has been all encompassing and exciting, often reflecting some of the facade concepts created for their Asian counterparts.

The in-house architectural team is led by Irish architect David McNulty and American architect Eric Carlson. The team's offices in Paris look like any other busy architectural studio; models, prototypes and sketches decorate the desks, tables and walls, and the environment is young and international. Other architectural studios in Paris, Verona and Tokyo are also part of the new set-up and make up the remaining five architects in the exhibition title. (20 per cent of store projects are designed internally and the remaining 80 per cent are managed by the Paris office using external architects.)

Louis Vuitton boasts the ownership and operation of over 300 stores worldwide, and continues to open or renovate between 50 and 100 new stores each year. Like the famed, iconic prints on its trunks and bags, the architecture of the stores is also reaching out to the public, reinforcing these icons in oversized 3-D form, and pitching them as desirable objects in this almost surrealist world. For example, the chequerboard pattern of toile Damier has been a source of reference for a number of locations; the Sapporo store uses a giant version of a similar geometrical pattern for its display windows; Seoul uses a translucent metal mesh to cover the facade with

Above: **Louis Vuitton Roppongi.** The exterior skin is composed of over 20,000 parallel glass tubes arranged as a vast pixelised screen

Right: **Louis Vuitton Roppongi.** The interior of the store has a distinctly high-tech feel to it, with references to the inside of a trunk. Fibre-optics are used in the stairs to project images. Traditional retail spaces are retained behind the patterned transparent walls that enclose the dancefloor zone of this club-like store

reference to the texture of the fabric covering many of the LV travel chests; and taking the metaphor into the design of the building, the Louis Vuitton store in Omotesando resembles a randomly stacked set of trunks. Architecture clearly has its own strategy: to house a world-class brand and invite the public to engage with that brand. And it does so with remarkable ingenuity.

One of the more recent projects, in Roppongi, Japan, is designed by Aurelio Clementi, Jun Aoki and Eric Carlson, and strives to respond directly to the constant developments and changes in the world of fashion. Like Prada in SoHo, the store establishes the brand in a younger, hipper area than you would normally expect. Conceived with a nightclub theme, the store created such anticipation that it had a queue of potential shoppers sleeping on the street the night before the opening. The facade is composed of over 20,000 parallel glass tubes arranged as a huge pixelised screen. This two-directional sculpture produces a blurring mirage effect. The interiors are high-tech and themed around the infamous nightlife of Roppongi, with bar, lounge and fibreoptic video dancefloors overlapping with traditional retail spaces.

Other completed and ongoing projects include Japanese ventures in Kobe, designed by Philippe Barthélémy and Sylvia Griño; Kochi, designed by Kumiko Inui; and Tokyo, by Kengo Kuma & Associates. Eric Carlson and David McNulty are responsible for outlets in Hawaii and Hong Kong, while Jun Aoki & Associates have designed a new New York store.

Presented here are some images of the recent architectural designs for the stores in Japan and Korea, and the interior designs of two of the stores in Europe and the US.

SPECTACULAR HOUSES

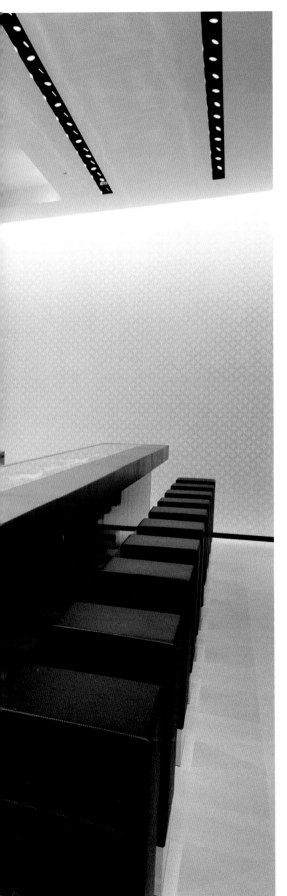

Left and above: **Louis Vuitton Roppongi.** The 'bag-bar' is designed like a series of stacked boxes. Blacks and whites are used as base colours, giving the scene very clean lines

Below: **Louis Vuitton Roppongi.** A view of the glass tube facade from within. The Louis Vuitton motif creates a texture for the white wall finishings

Left and above: **Louis Vuitton Nagoya.** The double skin of the building creates a vertical mist against which many displays could float. The external glass wall and the inner wall were both given the distinctive Louis Vuitton chequerboard Damier pattern, creating a hologram-type effect as a result

Right:
Louis Vuitton trunks

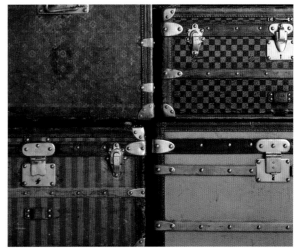

Right and left: Louis Vuitton Seoul.
The exterior is a double-layered facade composed of a Damier-patterned, mosaic-tiled shell wrapped by a stainless steel metal fabric. Non-luxurious materials are combined with rich textures, reminiscent of the classic Louis Vuitton steamer trunk

Above: Louis Vuitton SoHo, New York.
View of the exterior which typifies the
architecture of the city's hip zone

Right: Louis Vuitton SoHo, New York. These 1998
interiors reveal the flexibility of the architectural team –
they create a rich and luxurious palette of interior
design when structural redesign is prohibited

Below: **Louis Vuitton Paris.** Interior of the store on Avenue de Montaigne

Below: **Louis Vuitton Paris.** Completed in 2003, these interiors show the evolutionary development of the Louis Vuitton stores, distinct from New York, for example, where interior architectural elements start to feature much more

Architectural Branding

This series of project studies illustrates cases where the architect has been invited to develop an architectural concept for the brand name that may then act as a blueprint for the stores worldwide.

What emerges in this area of work are two points of interest: firstly, the synergy between the architect and the fashion designer; and secondly, the notion that an architectural concept can be relevant (or even desirable) at a global level, without being sensitive to location (just as fashion designs are aimed at a worldwide audience).

Dealing with the first issue and looking at our case studies, it is apparent that fashion designers have deliberately chosen architects whose built work can be identified with their own designs, or that they recognise that the architect's understanding of design is complementary to their own. It seems to come down to a very personal relationship between the fashion designer and the architect, and the union is one of personal tastes.

For example, Giorgio Armani, the world's leading minimalist fashion guru, chose Claudio Silvestrin, a fellow Italian and a leader in minimalist forms. Jil Sander seems to have found her architectural style with Michael Gabellini and

Architectural Branding

Gabellini Associates, whose work, although minimal, has a slightly rounded, feminine edge to it, mirroring the fine cut of Sander's clothes designs.

In all these cases, the architecture can be seen to be a direct extension of the fashion, where the styles of the garments find their home in built form. The store designs for Marni by Future Systems can also be seen to reflect the style of clothing, but pushed to the extremes of its ideas of colour and shape. The original concept by Jan Kaplicky of Future Systems was to be able to accommodate the seasonal changes of fashion in the interior architecture. There are other interesting relationships where the architect has confronted the more flamboyant fashion designs with a very calm, clean store environment with a hint of daring, allowing the garments and objects to sit harmoniously side by side. This can be said of Will Russell's designs for Alexander McQueen stores where an almost futuristic all-white environment houses exquisite and contemporary tailoring; and Future Systems' designs for Comme des Garçons that very much reflect the ideas of the fashion house.

Another case where the architect has really looked at fashion designs in depth in order to pursue a concept in architecture is Sophie Hicks Architects' design for Chloé. Sophie Hicks looked at the funky, fashionable and sexy image of Chloé and came up with an architectural concept that complemented the brand image, sometimes by playing on opposites, and carried that sensual, feminine edge into built form. Universal Design Studio's concept for the Stella McCartney stores also can be said to embody much of the designs and styles of Stella in its architectural interiors.

By contrast, a project by Italian-based architects Lazzarini Pickering, for Fendi, has turned to architectural form and the use of raw materials, rather than the fashion of the brand itself, to provide the setting for luxurious items.

Perhaps these stores want to reach beyond the garment and offer something more than just shoes, bags or clothes. By pairing up with architects who complement their style, the store starts to embody the idea of the brand and reinforces the style through solid form.

The second aspect to this work is the idea that the architect can develop a store concept that can be used as a worldwide blueprint for the fashion designer. While it is completely accepted that fashion can have resonance worldwide at the same moment in time, it has not always been the case that architectural styles can be 'globalised' in the same way. Many of the cases cited above involve architectural styles that have avoided translation into local architectural languages. Rather, the original design concept, which is established as true to the fashion brand, is followed in other countries. Silvestrin's stores for Giorgio Armani, for example, are almost identical in every city. This seems to work very well in reinforcing the brand concept globally and brings a sense of harmony to the brand wherever it finds itself. (Often these architects are also asked to design the concession the brand may have in larger department stores, continuing the theme in every instance.)

As a slight variation, the work for Fendi by Lazzarini Pickering is at least site-sensitive. Although very much in keeping with the fashion brand's designs, the architectural concepts respond to the individual sites. For example, Fendi Rome is located in a historical building and thus takes on the historical theme; Fendi Paris has a very distinct staircase and so the theme centres around this architectural feature; and so on.

By highlighting two or more stores designed by the same architect in the major fashion cities of London, Paris, New York, Milan and Tokyo, the nine projects presented in this chapter give a broad insight into the way a fashion brand can find its expression in architecture.

Claudio Silvestrin Architects

Giorgio Armani

Paris 1999
Milan 2000
São Paulo 2001
London 2003

Giorgio Armani and Claudio Silvestrin are two names that sit very well together, creating between them a harmonious reciprocity between clothing and architecture. Armani is one of the few international fashion houses that has remained a family business, and a very successful one at that. Part of its prosperity lies in its loyal commitment to a very distinct style of fashion that never seems to deviate too far. Known for sleek lines, minimalist fashions and his own token black uniform, Armani chose Claudio Silvestrin – minimalist, thoughtful, elegant, and also Italian – as the architect for his stores.

To date, Silvestrin has designed 30 Giorgio Armani stores worldwide, the first in Paris in 1999 and the most recent ones in Shanghai, Hong Kong and Seoul. The combination of Armani's clean lines and Silvestrin's own commitment to minimalism and elegance has resulted in spaces with a monastic air, where raw stone and beautiful cloth sit side by side. The stores are refined, simple and spatial, using exquisite materials – such as ebony, limestone and granite – to create a timeless quality, much like an art gallery. Suits and dresses hang almost solemnly in the stores, punctuating the length of the interior walls whose long lines are created through a very distinct lack of interruption by intersections and other materials.

The locations illustrated here – from the early stores of Paris and Milan through to the more recent ones of Vienna and London – may be distinguished by their location and exterior, but typically echo each other in their interior treatment, with a shared palette of materials, details and features reinforcing the identity of the international brand.

The global reach of Armani and the extent to which Silvestrin's store designs have been rolled out worldwide is reflected in the fact that in 2003 alone, he executed stores in Dubai, Atlanta, Busan, Rome, Barcelona and London. With more new stores planned, the Silvestrin/Armani partnership remains ongoing.

Above: **Armani Paris.** The entrance to the store is characterised by a large stone vessel, marking the pared-down approach to design found throughout the store

Below: Armani Paris. In the menswear department suits are hung quietly around an uncluttered ebony centrepiece. A standing light illuminates from behind, reflecting off the stone walls, whilst the signature square-lights sit neatly above the drawers

Right: Armani Paris. Lighting is used to create different zones in the most subtle way. Turning the corner from the entrance, ebony furnishings are introduced to complement the backdrop of limestone

Above: Armani Milan.
The length of the store is
accentuated by the Macassar
ebony ledge, onto which
shoes, bags and other
accessories are carefully
placed. Lighting is subtle
and elegant

Right: **Armani Milan.** The
entrance is defined by a subtly
lit pool of water, enhancing
the raw French limestone in
which it sits. The plain glass
facade maximises the use of
natural light, another feature
of Silvestrin's architecture

Above and below: **Armani Milan.**
The use of natural materials and the
lack of ornament give the space a
monastic-like quality. Spaces are
defined by elegant lines and forms

Left: Armani São Paulo. The exterior could easily be mistaken for a contemporary church with its solid stone walls and long elegant glimpses into the store. The long but shallow steps allow for a relaxed entrance lit by Silvestrin's signature square-lights

Right: Armani São Paulo. An exterior shot showing the solid stone walls interrupted only by lengths of glass reaching the height of the building

Below: Armani São Paulo. Inside, the natural light offers more straight lines amongst the contemporary and minimal furnishings

Above left and right: **Armani London.** The Sloane Street store is the latest in a series of flagship stores. The choice of materials, the design of the entrance hall and staircases, the use of natural light and the fluidity of the space are characteristic of Silvestrin's design concept for Giorgio Armani. The floor and the walls are clad in St Maximin limestone, with furniture in Macassar ebony and oxidised brass

Gabellini Associates

Jil Sander

Hamburg (Offices and Showroom) 1996
New York 2002

Gabellini Associates, based in New York, have worked on many high-fashion retail projects but have perhaps become best known for their refined, minimalist and elegant designs and restorations for the Jil Sander stores worldwide. Michael Gabellini's relationship with Jil Sander goes back to 1982 when he designed the Linda Dresner store in New York, which was then the only place where Sander's designs were available. He was invited by Sander to design her first store in Paris, 1993. Since then, Gabellini Associates have designed 31 stores for the brand worldwide, including the head office and showroom in Hamburg and the showroom in Milan, which in turn has included a variety of unique, historic restorations.

The Hamburg showroom opened in 1996 in a restored 19th-century landmark villa on the banks of Lake Alster. The building had sustained considerable damage during the Second World War and occupation by the German Finance Ministry, and so required extensive renovation and restoration, both interior and exterior. Gabellini's architectural solutions maintained the balance between old and new; plaster reliefs and woodwork complemented the bold reconfiguration of the interiors, which were filled with custom-made furnishings and fixtures; a new stairway to the lower level was added to the original grand staircase; and a terrace, formed as part of the excavations, connects the lower-level dining area to the surrounding park.

The New York flagship is a very large project that encompasses the entire six floors of the building to accommodate a showroom and offices. This project also entailed the reconfiguration of the limestone facade as a seamless and balanced composition that was also in keeping with neighbouring buildings. The interiors continue the historic reference with the warmth of the limestone floors and nickel silver display units alongside spare, ephemeral and floating interior structures. The space has been altered to afford a double-height entry and triple-height backlit stair atrium. Vertically accentuating this, the west wall unfolds through the three floors as both a display wall and an ambient light source. This particular interior feature also helps navigate the client from the front of the store to the back of the space.

Gabellini also designed a London flagship store for Jil Sander, but it closed amid losses during a difficult time for the label, when it was bought and sold again by Prada. The new owner, Change Capital, intends to open a new London flagship in the near future.

Above: Jil Sander Hamburg. View of the very grand 19th-century landmark villa on the banks of Lake Alster. The building had sustained considerable damage during the Second World War and occupation by the German Finance Ministry, and so required extensive renovation and restoration before it re-emerged as Jil Sander's head office and showroom

Right and below: **Jil Sander Hamburg.**
Gabellini's architectural solutions maintained the balance between old and new; plaster reliefs and woodwork were completely restored to their former elegance and a new contemporary stairway (below) to the lower level was added to complement the original grand staircase (right)

Left: Jil Sander New York. The interiors continue the historic reference of the facade, with the warmth of the limestone floors and nickel silver display units set alongside spare, ephemeral and floating interior structures. The space has been reconfigured to afford a double-height entry and triple-height backlit stair atrium

Left: Jil Sander New York. Minimalist and elegant, Gabellini's interiors for Jil Sander play on her own clean-cut design sensibilities. Nickel silver display units hold the minimum of items in this seemingly transitory environment

Above: **Jil Sander New York.** The ground and first floors feature accessories, women's ready-to-wear clothes and shoes; the second floor houses men's ready-to-wear and shoes

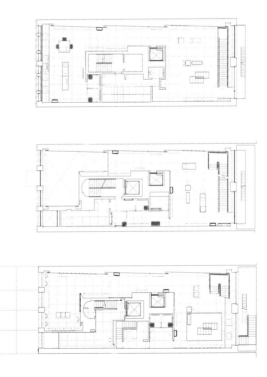

Right: **Jil Sander New York.** Floor plans

Universal Design Studio

Catriona MacKechnie

New York 2005

Universal Design Studio's store for luxury lingerie retailer Catriona MacKechnie has been developed to create a balance between its very masculine location on Manhattan's West 14th Street and the feminine nature of the merchandise. Jonathan Clarke, director of Universal Design Studio, says that the company 'wanted to create a store for women's lingerie that is properly designed for women'. Even though the store may be ostensibly just a small, rectangular boutique, and Catriona MacKechnie may not rate as one of the heavy hitters among Universal's roster of 'stella' clients, Clarke judges the finished design to be among the firm's most satisfying work. This is partly due to the good relationship between the client and the designer, with their aspirations working in tandem, but it must also be due to the design's capacity to surprise through the use of detail and material. As the New York store is MacKechnie's first boutique, it also gave Universal the opportunity to help establish the identity of the brand.

Given the nature of the products, there must have been a temptation to make the design thrill with frills, but, more cleverly, the walls form a transition phase between the hard external environment of the Meatpacking District and the delicacy of the wares. The glass entrance facade angles downwards and inwards from the original threshold of the rather ominous, iron-clad 19th-century building that houses the store. Picking up from the ironwork, black marble frames the glass, and inside other hard materials – steel, nickel, Corian, lacquered screens and timber – are used to create the mainstay of the design. However, the masculinity of the entrance is successfully dissolved into a variety of softer, warmer textures through the treatment of these materials. The box-like store is divided into two areas, with the main retail space separated from the brighter service and dressing room area by semi-translucent, backlit screens that echo the transparency of the merchandise and offer tantalising glimpses of softened shadows and colours.

The most significant use of texture to soften the harshness of the materials occurs in the display area's two outer walls, which are made of individually pressed and coloured small steel plates, establishing a variegated, almost pixelated, effect as a backdrop to the lingerie. A sculptured and curving white Corian wall creates a semi-partition and is also used as the store's most eye-catching display feature. Other items are displayed individually on white, handcrafted trays, on inverted hangers atop freestanding metal poles, or on a two-tier rail system that lines one wall. The wooden floor is stained dark to aid the seductive allure of the space.

The dressing rooms are less sultry, but frills are finally allowed to take their place in the form of a ceiling decorated with dense waves of white georgette

Above and opposite: Catriona MacKechnie New York. The left-hand and rear walls of the display area have a 'feathered' effect, created by individually made, rectangular steel panels. The design is full of variation in texture, with the impact of hard materials softened to form a backdrop to the delicate fabrics of the lingerie fabric. Screens are also used in the dressing rooms and are patterned with white floral reliefs that contribute to the subtle overall effect of an ethereal garden.

Universal's concept seems to draw strength from the determination of Catriona MacKechnie to create a powerful identity for her new brand, which focuses on bespoke, luxury designs from a range of international labels with sometimes limited presence in the US. The choice of merchandise has made this, the very first MacKechnie store, something of a New York destination. Universal has managed to give her space a very particular sense of its own branding, ensuring that it is complementary to the products while not being submerged by them. The practice's ability to do this within a standard rectangular box augurs well for the planned roll-out of further Catriona MacKechnie boutiques.

Left: Catriona MacKechnie New York. A curving Corian wall partitions the main space and is also used to highlight individual products

Opposite: Catriona MacKechnie New York. The dressing room area, with a georgette-covered ceiling and floral-relief panelling, is suggestive of a heavenly Oriental garden

Below: Catriona MacKechnie New York. The store's glass frontage slopes back from the building's iron-clad facade in New York's Meatpacking District

Above and opposite: **Catriona MacKechnie New York.** Render, sketches and plan of Universal Design Studio's concept

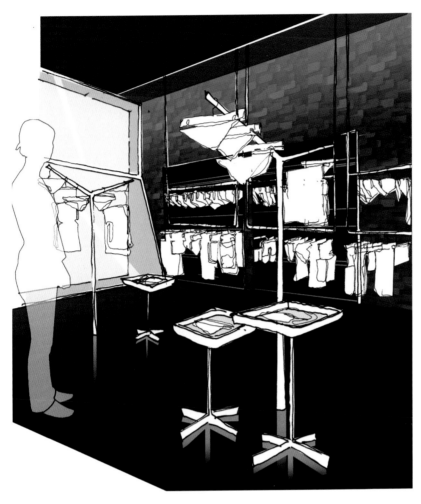

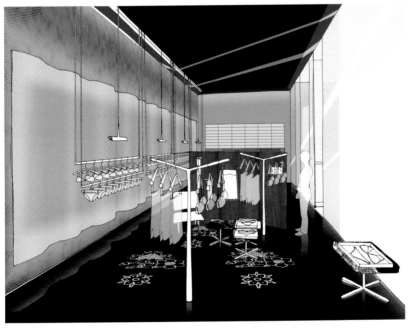

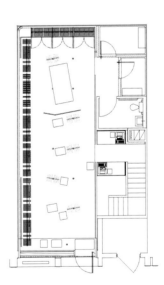

Lazzarini Pickering

Fendi

London 2001
Paris 2001
Rome 1998–2002

Fendi, now part of the Louis Vuitton Moët Hennessy group, is perhaps best known for its luxurious leather bags and accessories, as well as sumptuous garments. The design for the Fendi stores was a collaborative effort between Rome-based architects Lazzarini Pickering and Silvia Venturini Fendi, the creative director of the company. The main thrust was to create dark and luxurious architectural interiors rather than just filling the space with products and display units. The chosen display elements – shelves, tables and suspended horizontal and vertical units – are designed as architectural objects and their size is decided in proportion to the space. For example, shelves may be as long as 10 metres, tables 7 metres, and the suspended units up to 20 metres long.

The location of each store required a slightly different architectural configuration of the basic display units and Lazzarini Pickering made use of the differences by giving a theme to each of the different stores. In London it is the facade, in Paris the staircase, and in Rome the historic building. However, the Fendi stores are highly recognisable due to their common architectural components.

In London, the distinguishing feature is the facade where display windows form the entire frontage, framed by a smooth flush white Portland stone. In the absence of a traditional shop window, the whole store becomes the display as the passer-by can view it all from the street, while the customer also becomes part of the display. This lack of division between outside and inside is augmented by the way the interior reflects details of the merchandise. The dark backdrop allows the luxury garments and accessories to be projected or emphasised. The interior materials are 'impoverished': raw sheet metal for the floor and shelves, and a layered iron-based painted render for the wall panel system and hanging volumes. The configuration of the display units is almost sculptural and at the same time informal, encouraging the client to touch or try on, and not feel overwhelmed with the formality of architectural form.

The Paris store pivots around the staircase which is a vortex of display elements that encourages clients to move from one floor to another. It is an enormous structure on which clothes, accessories, shoes and bags are placed. The use of traditional low-tech materials (as in London) has allowed for some variation; rendered surfaces are finished with an iron-based paint often used to protect metal surfaces, giving a wax finish to treated crude iron.

Lazzarini Pickering has also designed stores for Fendi in Bologna, New York, Sydney and Bangkok.

Above: **Fendi Paris.** A long view of the store

Right: **Fendi Paris.** The design of the store pivots around the staircase

Above: **Fendi Paris.** Stand-alone furnishings are
used to distinguish other zones of the store

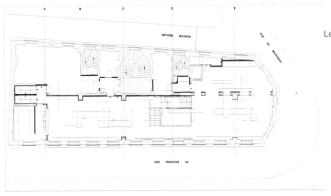

Left: **Fendi Paris.** Ground-floor plan

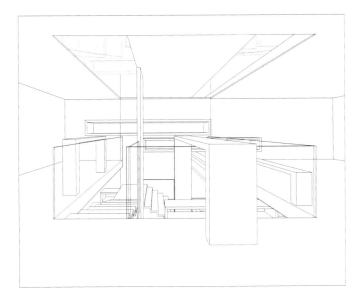

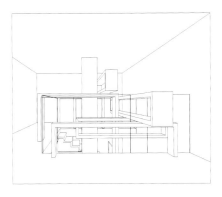

Above left and above: **Fendi Paris.** Architectural drawings

Above: **Fendi London.** The client inside the store can become part of the display. The signature architectural forms used by Lazzarini Pickering are also part of the facade

Left: **Fendi London.** In the absence of a traditional shop window the entire store becomes the display as the passer-by can view the whole space from the street

Above and opposite, top: **Fendi London.** The interiors are given a dark backdrop and the materials are deliberately 'impoverished' in comparison to the luxury goods: raw sheet metal for the floor and shelves, and a layered iron-based painted render for the wall panel system and hanging volumes. The configuration of the display units is almost sculptural and at the same time informal enough not to be intimidating

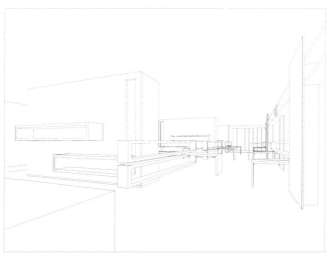

Left: **Fendi London.**
Architectural drawings

Right: **Fendi London.**
Plans

Above and right: **Fendi Rome**. The dominant theme
is its historic features. The signature architectural
display forms are perfectly fitting for these vaulted
Italian rooms, and also sit alongside video panels
that bring the old and the new face to face

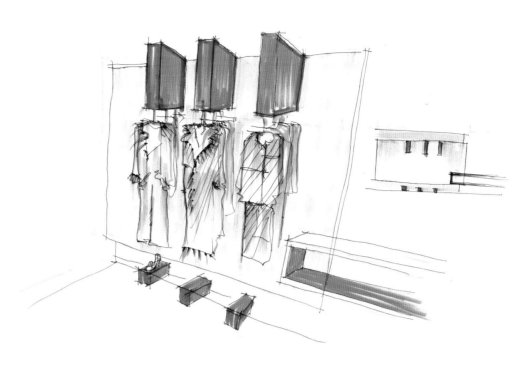

Above and below: **Fendi Rome.** Concept sketches

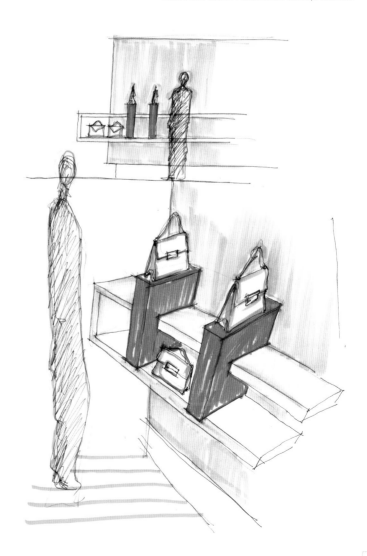

Left: **Fendi Rome.** Fendi's
trademark display units intersect
the space

Future Systems

Comme des Garçons

New York 1998
Tokyo 1998
Paris 1999

Comme des Garçons initiated a collaboration with Future Systems in a number of different city locations. The brief was to create a new kind of space with an atmosphere of experimentation that has resulted in a powerful, uncompromising environment. The relationship between the space and the clothing is dictated by the design, its vision and the undiluted expression of the will to take risks.

The New York store, which opened in a former warehouse in 1998, is located in West Chelsea which is not an established designer retail area. Rather, it is home to many large, modern art galleries, several of which were designed by Richard Gluckman. The art crowd make it a vibrant place to be in the evenings and the clever positioning and design of the Comme des Garçons store ensure that visitors to gallery events easily seep into it. Perhaps this smooth synthesis between fashion retail and the local, cultural environment partly inspired Rem Koolhaas's vision for Prada SoHo.

Rather than create an entirely new facade, Future Systems retained the 19th-century fabric of the warehouse with all its old signage and external industrial fire escapes. Grafted behind the central existing brickwork, the entrance arch provides the link to the store. Juxtaposing the old with the new, the arch frames an asymmetrical, tubular entrance structure made entirely from aluminium. This link transports the individual from the streets of New York into the Comme des Garçons environment. The tube structure becomes an in-between space, neither of the day nor of the night, and not really either inside or outside. Instead, it is a fissure through an existing building into a new and challenging environment. The result is a calm yet unusual space, punctuated by a single row of marker lights. The skin of the tube has been mechanically formed and then finished by hand.

In the 1998 design for the Tokyo store, two horizontal concrete slabs of a dumb, existing building are joined with two ribbons of conically curved, inclined glass offering a simple liquid entrance at the point where they converge. The glass is covered with a layer of translucent blue dots which acts as a filter between interior and exterior. At night the movement of people within the shop creates a curiosity for the pedestrian passing the facade.

The Paris store, which opened in 1999, is the third in this series. The brief was to design a shop which was to be dedicated entirely to perfume. The historic, worn, stone facade is both protected and enhanced by a sheer skin of pale pink glass which slides gracefully in front of it.

Above and opposite, below: **Comme des Garçons New York.** View of the West Chelsea store from the street. The 19th-century red brick facade was retained in complete contrast to the design of the interior

Above: **Comme des Garçons New York.** The view through the tunnel into the store. Stepping into this tube from the street, with its low height and rippling texture, makes the transformation from one world to the next immediate and all encompassing

Above: **Comme des Garçons New York.**
Detail of the tunnel and the entrance door

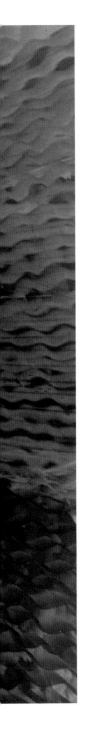

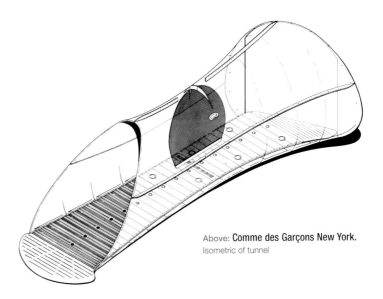

Above: **Comme des Garçons New York.**
Isometric of tunnel

Below: **Comme des Garçons New York.** Viewed from inside the store, the tube looks like a mouth gaping onto the real world

Opposite, top and left: **Comme des Garçons Tokyo.** Two horizontal concrete slabs of an existing building are joined with two ribbons of conically curved, inclined glass, offering a simple liquid entrance where they converge

Above, top and bottom: **Comme des Garçons Tokyo.** The glass is covered with a layer of translucent blue dots which act as a filter between interior and exterior. At night the movement of people within the shop creates a curiosity for the pedestrian passing the facade

Above: **Comme des Garçons Paris.** View of
the elevation of the store in Paris, dedicated to
selling perfume

Above: **Comme des Garçons Paris.**
Elevation detail from street

Future Systems

Marni

Milan 1999
London 1999
New York 2001
Paris 2001

In the late 1990s, Future Systems, the Czech-Anglo partnership of Jan Kaplicky and Amanda Levete was asked to create a design concept for Marni stores and their concessions within department stores. Marni's colourful, eclectic fashion collections found their perfect match with Future Systems, known for its contemporary use of high-tech materials and organic forms.

Work for Marni, and indeed other creations for retail spaces (see Comme des Garçons and Selfridges profiles in this book), revolutionised ideas for store designs and stamped Future Systems' name into the fashion world in bold letters. Curvaceous and playful, Future Systems' designs are thought-provoking, questioning architecture's creative use and design of space. In a retail context such as this, it initiates innovation in the choreography of display and, specifically, how clothes hang on rails. Its work is the opposite of minimalism, deploying mostly synthetic, disposable materials and carving up the shop space with curves, arches, disks and islands.

The spirit of the stores has been generated by the clothes themselves, resulting in a composition where the store and clothes are part of one landscape. The concept was to present the clothes on a sculptural white island which sits against the brightly coloured backdrop of the rest of the shop. The original concept by Jan Kaplicky was to be able to accommodate the seasonal changes of fashion in the interior architecture by changing the coloured backdrop. The curved shape of the island is literally reflected by a mirrored stainless steel ceiling of the same shape, transforming the plan of the rectilinear shop into a space with depth and height. The background colour can be chosen to suit a particular collection and can be varied with changing seasons to give a fresh look.

Selected clothes and accessories are displayed on tall, delicate stainless steel branches or, in shops where height is limited, from stainless steel ceiling hooks. Clothes are also displayed from a stainless steel rail (which curves around the perimeter of the island), a dynamic element that changes from being a hanging rail to a flat surface for display, and then a serving counter. The clothes are hung on specially made plexiglass hangers, designed by Future Systems to be sculptural elements within the overall shop design. Unlike a traditional solution, these hang below the rail which reads as a continuous, sinuous line.

(In August 2003, the store on Sloane Street featured here was closed and Marni reopened in larger premises a few doors down. The original scheme was 'reworked' by Sybarite. This newly imported design team are now working with Marni on an ongoing basis.)

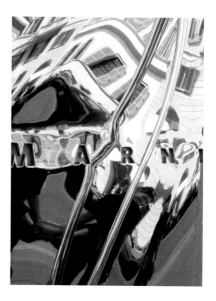

Above: **Marni Milan.** In typical Future Systems style, the door of Marni Milan plays on light, colour and reflections by using a sheet of curved steel from top to bottom

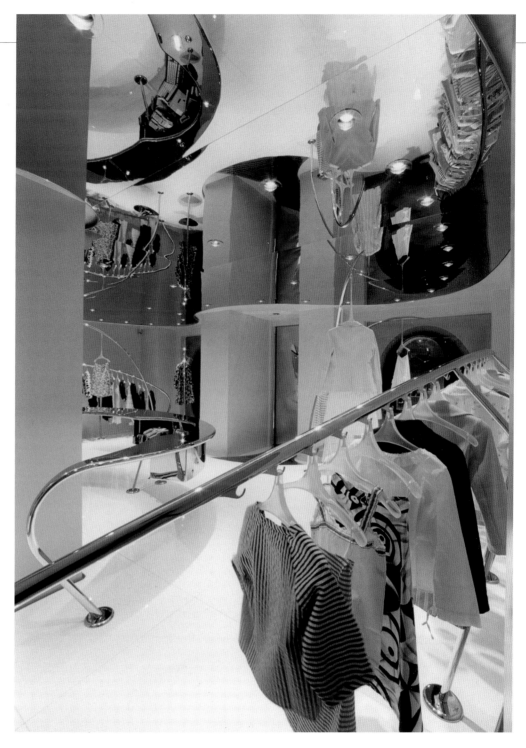

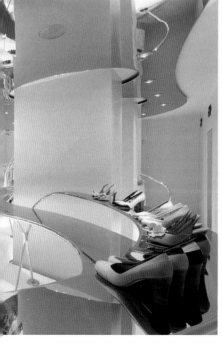

Above: **Marni Milan.** Detail of the clothes rail that literally wraps around the store, following the circular pathways of the walls

Left: **Marni Milan.** The white island reflected in the mirrored ceiling completely challenges the rectilinear plan of the shop, carving the space up with waves of clothes rails and curves of shoes. In the background are the round shop windows onto the street, shaping the view into the store

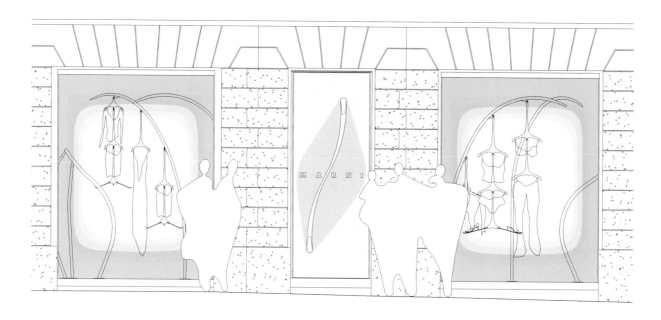

VIA S . ANDREA

Above: Marni Milan. Detail of a drawing of
the front elevation

Above: Marni Milan. Street elevation with views
into the store via the 'eyeballs'

Above: **Marni London.** View of the Marni store from the street at night. (All London images are prior to the 2003 refit)

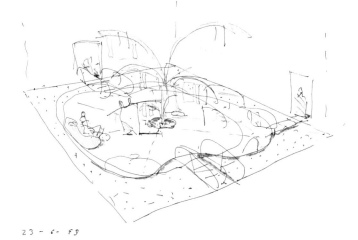

23 - 6 - 89

Left: **Marni London.** Concept sketch by founding partner of Future Systems, Jan Kaplicky

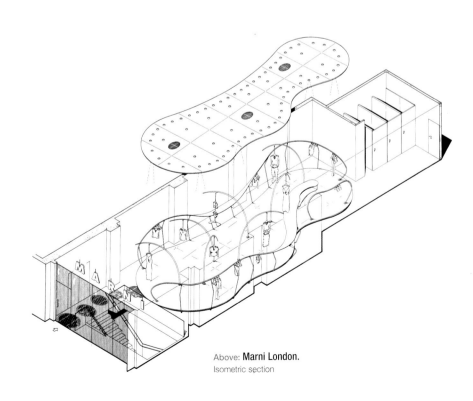

Left: **Marni London.** Long view of store, with the curves of the rails playfully carving up the blue interior, and bouncing off the mirrored ceiling

Above: **Marni London.** The clothes rail continues around the interior of the shop, wrapping its way around walls and floor

Above: **Marni London.**
Isometric section

Left: **Marni New York.** Viewed from the street, the store has had to fit into a more pre-defined space than London or Milan, with original features of the building sitting alongside Future Systems' reflective and curving design solutions

Left: **Marni New York.** A long view of the interior. With its pristine white backdrop, the store seems even more space-age than the other colourful stores of Milan or London

Left: **Marni Paris.** The store opens out with its curved white island floor and ceiling. The sinuous curves of the stainless steel display rails have been further developed to incorporate three levels of accessory shelves

Below: **Marni Paris.** The display rails sprout from the floor like trees

Above: **Marni Paris.** Reflections of rails and garments in the mirrored ceiling create height and depth to an otherwise typical store space

Above: **Marni Paris.** Detail of one of the curved
display rails with hangers also designed by
Future Systems

Sophie Hicks Architects

Chloé

London 2002
Hong Kong 2006

London-based Sophie Hicks Architects was asked to develop the concept for the new Chloé stores along with the company's artistic director, Phoebe Philo. Chloé, the brand, is known for its sexy, young and luxurious designs, with a slightly provocative attitude. It gave Stella McCartney her big break when she was still fresh out of college, employing her as chief designer before she fled to Gucci and established her own brand. Sophie Hicks Architects were briefed to encapsulate and evoke the spirit of Chloé's designs in the stores.

Philo wanted the stores to be light and airy, and the first design, on London's Sloane Street, achieved this through the use of an all-glass frontage, pale materials and very fragile shelving. However, the atmosphere of the store is more casual than formal. Touches of the boudoir, including gold-plated clothes rails, contrast with huge black speakers and plywood walls.

The entire design thrives on such contrasts. The display tables have salmon marble veneer tops resting on gold-plated legs, but the tops are so unusually thin and the legs are trestles, thereby managing to conjure a cheap and temporary effect from luxurious materials. The shoes are displayed on delicate shelving that faces bulky white seating. The airiness of the space is aided by the use of light-diffusing screens that merely suggest different areas, but this gives way to the dark solidity of the fitting rooms, which have low ceilings and are clothed in black satin.

The lighting is designed as for a museum space, using spotlights to model or flood the clothes just as one would a picture or a sculpture. At night, only the mannequins and glass screens are illuminated for dramatic effect.

The door handle to the store carries Chloé's signature piece – a sculpted bronze horse in full gallop – which is to be found on every door of every store.

All in all, the new architectural concept does seem to highlight the image that Chloé wishes to portray: touches of luxury with elements of street, non-threatening style with a surprising sliver of cool.

Based on the Sophie Hicks Architects blueprint, subsequent stores have opened in the premium locations of Madison Avenue in New York, Avenue Montaigne in Paris, and at the Mandarin Hotel in Hong Kong. These latest ventures feature a beautiful spiral staircase fashioned out of rough-cast concrete, adding to the contrast of luxury materials and unfinished surfaces.

Above: **Chloé London.** A concept sketch by Sophie Hicks Architects of the fitting rooms for the flagship store

Right: **Chloé London.** Concept sketch of display areas

Below: **Chloé London.** The facade gives a clean and contemporary feel with the token bronzed horse as the door handle, Chloé's signature statement on its own strong style

Above and left: Chloé London. The elegant and funky fashions are displayed with a backdrop of cheap plywood – the sort that would be used to board up the store in the event of a street demonstration. The salmon-coloured tabletop is so slim and delicate, it looks almost fragile resting on its gold-plated trestles. Mirrors lean against walls and furniture is freestanding

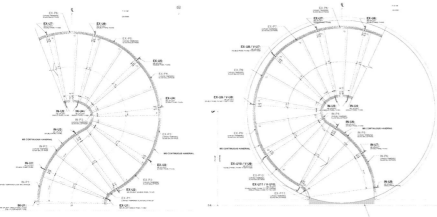

Above: **Chloé Hong Kong.** Since the initial London blueprint, Sophie Hicks has developed a rough-cast concrete spiral staircase as a focal point for the more recently designed Chloe outlets

Left: **Chloé New York.** Drawings of the spiral staircase

Will Russell

Alexander McQueen
New York 2002

Alexander McQueen, now part of the Gucci group, invited Will Russell to develop a design concept for his own brand stores that would be as distinctive as his line, and yet act as a blueprint for the outlets worldwide. Both London graduates, both London based, and both young and innovative, it seems that McQueen found his architectural match in Russell.

McQueen is just short of being known as the *enfant terrible* of fashion, with his daring, theatrical ideas that seem to find their form in exquisite tailoring; Russell, former partner of David Adjaye, is emerging from London's East End as one of the city's leading contemporary designers.

Russell looked at the project as producing an 'environment' for the brand that could be dropped in whether at flagship level or as a concession in a larger outlet. The store had to reflect the apparent contradictions in McQueen's designs – where the old meets the new, the soft with the sharp – while also being 'submissive' to the clothes themselves. McQueen was very much present in the architectural development, pushing for themes that were far from the slick modernist detail found in some retail environments, and leaning towards incorporating warm, curved and magical elements.

The New York store is in the up-and-coming Meatpacking District of Manhattan, where numerous bars and young designers' boutiques are mushrooming. The building is a former meat-packing warehouse that provides a wide and deep open space on a single floor. As such, the store required a focal point on entering, which was achieved with a 'mothership' – a torus-formed hanging display unit which discreetly houses the fitting rooms. The white, reflective interior takes on a space-age quality as display elements appear to lose their solidity and look like fabrics as curve merges with curve. Russell conceived of the shop subtractively, as a solid block of homogenous white material from which the spaces were then carved. Light-fittings were integrated within the display elements, leaving the ceiling and wall uninterrupted from other materials. The terrazzo floor also became a continuous, resinous surface rather than being carved up by tiles.

The hanging display cabinets are modular and able to be repeated in each store environment. However, the sculpted wall and ceiling surface are more freeform and dependent on the given space.

All the stores, including London, retain these labyrinthine qualities – even more so on the ground floor in Milan where the ceiling height is especially low (due to structural restrictions) and the store is divided into many smaller spaces. London is also split over two levels, where the staircase to the lower

Above: **Alexander McQueen New York.**
Accessories such as shoes and bags are beautifully placed as though objects in a gallery, carefully lit from within the display unit and reflected in mirrors opposite

Above: **Alexander McQueen New York.** Detail of the torus hanging display unit or 'mothership'. There are two entrances and a central hall of mirrors

level is the architectural focal point of the store. The staircase, an object in its own right, adds 'drama' to the store by giving a visual contact with the lower level. Milan's staircase is terrazzo and exhibits exquisite attention to detail – each step 'licks' the stairwall as it meets it with an upward stroke.

Being part of a larger parent holding group gave additional support to the work: Russell acknowledges that he worked closely with the Gucci Store Planning Department who have extensive knowledge of retail design for the whole of the Gucci group. Russell also designed the Alexander McQueen store in Tokyo, which opened in 2001.

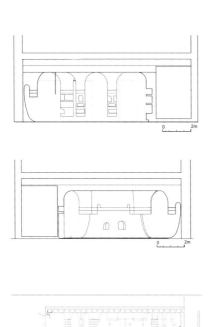

Above and below: Alexander McQueen New York. Plans and sections

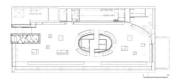

Right: Alexander McQueen New York. The interior of the store is unusually deep, being a former warehouse. The space is divided into smaller units, where the unit becomes the space and almost merges into one sinuous line of white. Garments and accessories are neatly placed in the environment and decorate the view with the only instances of colour

Above: **Alexander McQueen New York.** The
garments offer themselves up as navigational tools
in this long, white, ethereal space

Above: **Alexander McQueen New York.** The smooth and continuous terrazzo floor comes into its own, acting as a lighting board for the hidden display unit illumination. This configuration of lights and mirrors gives a futuristic feel to this gallery-type space

Universal Design Studio

Stella McCartney

New York 2002
London 2003

On graduating from Central St Martin's College of Art and Design in London, Stella McCartney walked straight into the chief designer job at Chloé and was swiftly offered her own brand within the Gucci group. The faith of Tom Ford, who also brought Alexander McQueen into the Gucci fold, was rewarded when her designs received almost unanimous approval and interest worldwide. The next step was to create her own stores along with the similarly youthful, London-based, and successful Universal Design Studio.

Common to each store is the idea of a space which will give respite from the hustle and bustle of the city – a calm and welcoming place to breathe. The first to open was the New York flagship store in 2002 in a converted warehouse on West 14th Street. The theme of an abstract landscape was developed by Universal Design Studio to create a warm and inviting atmosphere. The floor has contours and levels like a natural landscape from which clients can casually explore while the window display is set in a serene expanse of water with lily-esque display structures. The fitting rooms are hand-finished with an embroidered wall-covering designed by McCartney.

The London store, which opened a year later, is housed in a Grade II listed Georgian townhouse on Bruton Street, near Bond Street. Formerly an art gallery, the building underwent extensive refurbishments to create 6,000 square feet of retail space along with McCartney's London headquarters. The store manages to be both domestic and airy, while carrying touches of restored Georgian grandeur. The main room on the ground floor features a wall of inlaid and bejewelled designs which pick up on a nature theme that begins with the flooring. The room leads to a small but light-filled, glass-covered courtyard, and on to a back-room covered with a seemingly Georgian wallpaper, which on closer inspection reveals a rather menacing fairy-tale scene designed by McCartney. Upstairs the atmosphere is redolent of the rooms of a French couturier, but all sense of the past is juxtaposed with modern elements such as contemporary furniture. The feel of the store is eclectic and very personal.

Above: **Stella McCartney New York.** View of the store from West 14th Street

Above: **Stella McCartney New York.** The window
display has a water-like setting, reflecting the
mannequins as if from a pool of still water

Above: Stella McCartney New York. A wide view of the interior. This vast former warehouse now offers warmth and comfort in a zone that feels far from the crowded streets. The floor contours and levels like an abstract landscape

Right: Stella McCartney New York. Bags and shoes sit comfortably with vases of green and white. Designed by Universal Design Studio, contemporary pieces of furniture complement the themed space and fashion style

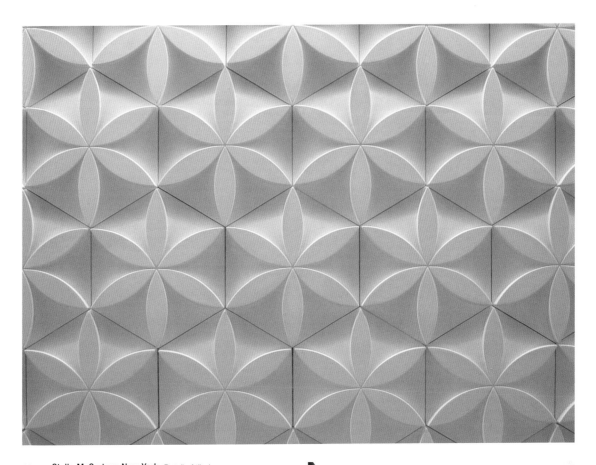

Above: **Stella McCartney New York.** Detail of tiled wall featuring three-dimensional tiles, inspired by the hexagon

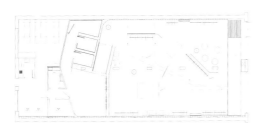

Above: **Stella McCartney New York.**
Ground-floor plan

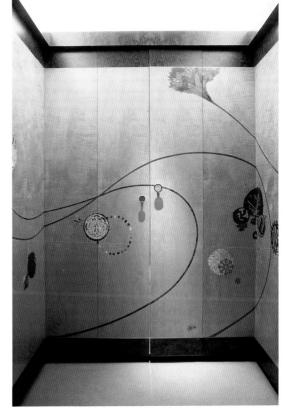

Right: **Stella McCartney New York.** Detail of the wall covering of handpainted fabric designed by Stella McCartney, incorporating the theme of abstracted nature

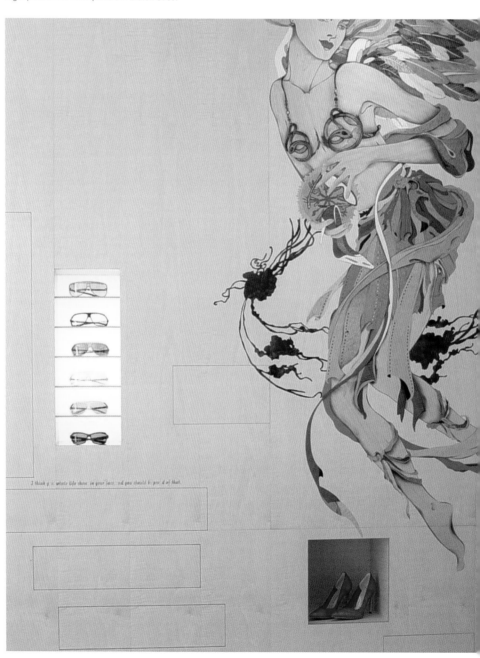

Left: **Stella McCartney London.** View of the flagship store and headquarters in Bruton Street

Above & right: **Stella McCartney London.** Views of the ground-floor interior. The marquetry decoration reflects the store's theme of nature with trees, branches and roots, and a fairy-like illustration designed by Stella McCartney runs across the walls

Left: **Stella McCartney London.** The glossy pink counter adds a feminine lightness to the woodland scene on the ground floor

Left & above: **Stella McCartney London.** Mannequins stand in front of the 3-D tiled walls that look on to the rear patio garden

Above: **Stella McCartney London.** Elements of
the former Mayfair townhouse are still obvious in the
architectural details. The fireplace and original
stucco give the store a very definite London feel

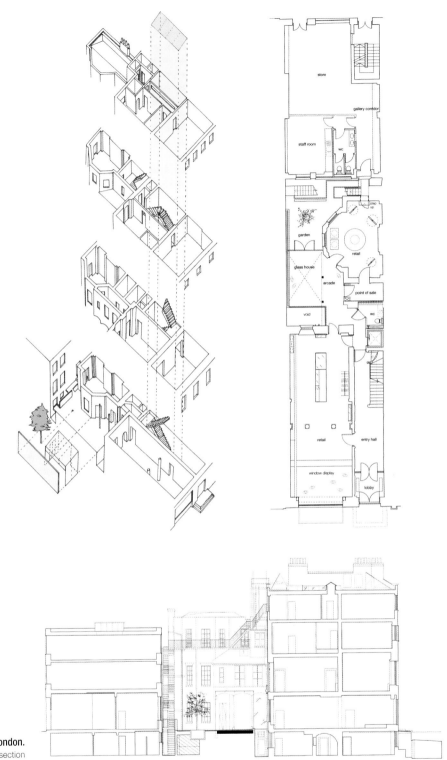

This page: **Stella McCartney London.**
Axonometric drawing, plan and section

Custom Made

When a fashion house requires a 'one-off' design solution for a store, often the strongest design element that emerges is formed by the architect's response to the location, which is then merged with their creative reaction to the particular fashion brand.

Each of the following projects, which are located in cities as diverse as Paris, Hong Kong, Milan, Seoul, Tokyo, London and New York, is a distinctive piece of interior architecture that reflects a bit of the city (or even the street) in which it is located. Some projects may be for a large international fashion house such as Burberry or Armani, while others are for slightly smaller but just as internationally acclaimed names such as Paul Smith and Issey Miyake.

Fuksas and Fuksas' work for Emporio Armani, daring and exciting as it is, also reflects the dare and excitement of Hong Kong's ultimate consumerist culture. This incredibly creative design uses the idea of the red ribbon, unfurling through the space, as used by Chinese gymnasts (and which is also a very strong symbol in Communist countries). The ribbon is used as the dominating architectural sculpture that shapes the navigation of this vast store.

Custom Made

In contrast, the designs by the Manhattan-based contemporary architects Janson Goldstein have given Emporio Armani a very different feel to their New York stores. Taking as source the neighbourhood within which it is located, the early SoHo store established a cool grey palette, using raw but smooth materials, that has carried through to the design for the subsequent Madison Avenue store.

In the case of Virgile and Stone, who have designed the first Italian store for Burberry, both British and Italian sentiments are embodied. Burberry, the fashionable brand that carries the great British traditions of the mackintosh raincoat, the umbrella and its signature plaid check, has ingrained its Britishness in its new Milan store through the interior architecture. Virgile and Stone have sensitively brought this Britishness in line with the elegant Milanese environment, resulting in a contemporary but classy store.

Sophie Hicks Architects, who designed two stores for another British design house, Paul Smith, shows its sensitivity to location whilst retaining a sense of continuity in its approach to Paul Smith's eclectic collections. In both London and Milan, the stores are located in grand houses and the original structural features of the interior have not only been retained but emphasised, respective to their host cultures: the domestic grandeur of the London townhouse, and the heights and vaults of the Milanese palazzo.

Projects in Asia include Cho Slade's designs for the Martine Sitbon store in Seoul, which also integrates its designs in the existing architecture, but chooses to respond more to the barn than to the former French villa. Curiosity's work with Gwenael Nicolas for Issey Miyake is slightly different in that the emphasis of the design is on the fashion brand rather than the location. However, references are made to each city's specific location – in Paris it is the grey brick street, in Tokyo it responds to the upmarket shopping district Aoyama.

6a and Tom Emerson introduce a completely new approach to interior design for fashion, just as the whole notion of 'shopping' is challenged by Oki-ni. The traditional transaction that takes place in the shop is no more, and instead all purchases are done via the Internet. What place, then, does the store have in this trade-free environment? 6a and Emerson have created a very casual store structure where both clients and store assistants can feel at ease and not at all overwhelmed by the brand.

Two other projects that only just fit into the title 'Custom Made' are those by Gabellini Associates. These projects represent more the way forward for certain types of fashion houses where the fashion goes beyond garments and accessories and enters into that all-encompassing concept of 'lifestyle'. Gabellini Associates' design for the Nicole Farhi store in New York also includes a restaurant that seems as important as the store itself; and the Gianfranco Ferré store in Milan has a spa (though not designed by Gabellini Associates). Distinguished, then, by its extensions (restaurant or spa), the brand not only reinforces its identity through interior form, but also through other activities.

Heatherwick Studio

Longchamp
New York 2006

British designer Thomas Heatherwick has established a worldwide reputation for tremendously innovative, technically extraordinary design solutions and sculptures, including the 56-metre *B of the Bang* in Manchester, the eight-storey high *Bleigiessen* sculpture for the Wellcome Trust Headquarters in London, and the Rolling Bridge. The latter is a hydraulic bridge across a London canal which, when not in use, curls up into a ball on one side of the water and reveals Heatherwick Studio's capacity for invention and lateral thinking. One of the studio's smaller projects was the 2003 Zip Bag, which became a great success for Longchamp. The leather bag is mostly made up of a continuous spiralling zip, which when unzipped allows the colourful inner lining to double the bag's depth and totally alter the design effect. When Longchamp, a family-run luxury accessories firm, decided to launch a New York flagship store on a problematic site, it turned to Heatherwick once more to provide an unlikely design solution.

Situated in SoHo, Spring Street may be a good site for a large flagship store, but the almost 930-square-metre property that Longchamp had secured came with the huge disadvantage of being above ground level, with other shops situated below, in a rather dull 1936 building. Heatherwick needed to draw customers up from the street. From Prada SoHo to the newest Chloé stores, staircases are being used more and more to provide the focal drama of high-end retail design, where space is at such a premium that the brand cannot afford 'dead' areas above or below the access level. The need to draw attention to hidden levels is even more acute for a store without the on-street window displays and direct level access that increase visibility and draw in passing trade. Heatherwick Studios describes its solution as a 'landscape' rather than a staircase.

The Longchamp site comprises three floors from a small ground-floor entranceway, up to the shop level and on to a new third floor containing offices, a showroom and a roof garden. A section was cut through the entire height of the building to create an 18-metre-tall atrium lit by a glass skylight that would lead customers upwards to the retail floor. The sculptural landscape runs from the entrance at the bottom of the lightwell and flows in contours like ribbons up through the floors and towards the skylight. The ribbons separate into individual strands to form the steps of the staircase and realign as a plane to create landings and then a wall as the structure leads towards the light. Consequently, the journey up to the store becomes a piece of theatre, full of expectation and adventure, which belies the extent of the engineering feat: the work took six months to construct from 55 tonnes of

Above: **Longchamp New York.** Overview of the 'landscape' staircase that draws customers up from a small entrance to the first-floor retail level

Below: **Longchamp New York.** The balustrades feature draping, contoured glass to suit the flow of the 'landscape'

Right: **Longchamp New York.** The 'landscape' is made up of 30 ribbons constructed from 55 tonnes of 30-millimetre rolled steel plate

hot-rolled steel. Unfortunately, necessary balustrades do fracture the flow of the sculpture, but Heatherwick developed glass panels (borrowing from aeroplane windshield technology) that he says 'drape like fabric' to suit the contoured landscape.

Heatherwick was keen for the architecture of the building to provide most of the store's display function, rather than rely on extra furnishings that would break the flow. Strips of laminated ash timber peel down from the ceiling to create the integrated display stands, with further layers flaying off from the stands to form the shelves. The sense of peeling is extenuated by the holes that the strips leave in the skin of the ceiling, revealing the building's service components. The building's original brick walls and cast-iron columns add to the stripped-back design that allows the products to dominate. Further freestanding display surfaces blend with the maple floor to ensure that they do not upset the architectural harmony of the display.

Detractors of high fashion may decry its superficiality, which does sometimes extend to even the most noteworthy designs of boutiques, but Heatherwick Studio has managed to give the Longchamp store an architectural credibility, beyond veneer, by allowing the structure of the building work to be the showpiece. It seems to be a perfect match for Longchamp, a non-flouncy Parisian firm that has been making high-quality luxury goods since 1948 and prides itself on the structural craftsmanship of its handbag designs.

Opposite: Longchamp New York. Strips of timber from the laminate ash ceiling are bent downwards to the floor to create the main display units

Right and below: Longchamp New York. Freestanding rectangular display units blend in with the maple flooring. The original brickwork and cast-iron columns have been left exposed, adding a touch of Manhattan-loft style

Above and right: **Longchamp New York.** Both the surface and underside of the ribbon landscape are used to display Longchamp bags

Opposite: **Longchamp New York.** The landscape ribbons separate to form the steps into the 418-square-metre retail floor before converging to create a wall up to the skylight

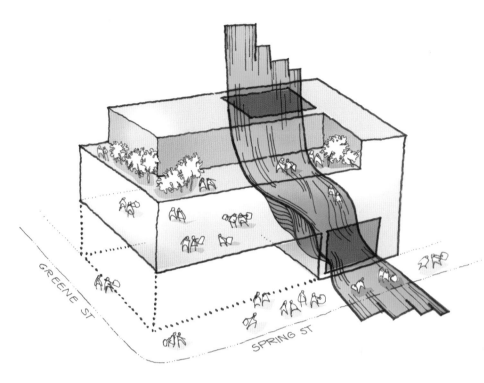

Above: Longchamp New York. Drawing of the staircase landscape flowing through the layers of the building

Left: Longchamp New York. Exterior of the 1936 building on the corner of Spring Street and Green Street in New York's SoHo

Below: Longchamp New York. Thomas Heatherwick's collaboration with Longchamp started in 2003 with the Zip Bag, which incorporates a spiralling zip which, when released, allows the inner layer to increase the depth of the bag. The design is suggestive of the steel ribbons that create the store's stairway

Marc Newson with
Sébastien Segers

Azzedine Alaïa

Paris 2006

Azzedine Alaïa's new accessories showcase in Paris is a temple for shoe fetishists. It is a serene, nearly circular space that is almost entirely free of extraneous furniture. It is all about the shoes, displayed just below eye level in recessed cabinets set into the curving wall: the room focuses purely on Alaïa's creations in a setting designed to inspire silent reverence. It is remarkable that this dignified hymn to quietude is separated from the rue de Moussy by just a set of glass doors. The store is designed by Marc Newson along with architect Sébastien Segers. Newson, the world-renowned Australian designer, is perhaps more famous as a household object designer, but he ventured into fashion boutique interiors as early as 1992 with the Claudia Skoda store in Berlin, and also developed a retail system for the W&LT streetwear label.

The circular design of the Alaïa store may orientate the eye towards the wares, but the interior structure is a paean to restrained luxury. The floor and walls are lined with white Carrara marble, the grey veins of which give the space its subtle texture. The marble slabs extenuate the concentric design, radiating out from a central circle, and curve upwards at the edge of the room to smooth away the join of floor and wall. Rising up from the floor is the only feature that breaks the flow: a structural column that ascends through the five storeys of the building. It has been integrated into the design by an encasement of two sections of marble. The lower block fans out to create a circular banquette – the only seating in the store. This is covered by six calfskin cushions, described as flesh coloured (which holds true if you happen to be a lightly tanned Caucasian). The marble pillar rises into a plain white plaster ceiling, but draws the eye towards one of the design's other concentric features – a large light that forms a ceiling recess. Light floods in between thin brass fins that join the inner and outer rims – Newson describes the fitting as like 'a brass Meccano'. Brass is also used for other fittings, including the banquette cushion studs and the custom-made LED spotlights in the display cases.

The true purpose of the 'flesh-coloured' calfskin becomes obvious within the 12 display cases. These are fully upholstered in the natural leather so that the colours of the shoes, boots and accessories are already set against the familiar hue of skin. The inner shelving of the cases is glass so there is no detraction from this tonal relationship.

Other than the glass doors on to the rue de Moussy, a second exit point is up seven steps, also clad in white Carrara marble, into Azzedine Alaïa's principle showroom, which has been separately designed. Alaïa, once known

Above: Azzedine Alaïa Paris. The single room, designed to showcase Azzedine Alaïa's shoes and accessories, is a simple, Bianco Carrara marble-clad circle

Above: **Azzedine Alaïa Paris.** The large, recessed ceiling light features a circle of brass fins

Right: **Azzedine Alaïa Paris.** The concentric design, cut into a difficult, angular space, features a central column, but no other interruptions. Marble covers an iron support pillar to integrate it within the design

as the 'king of cling' for the way his dresses caressed the body, was born in Tunis and studied sculpture before joining the Paris fashion industry and setting up his own label. In the mainstay his clothing designs could be described as 'sculptural minimalism', which is a description that also suits Newson and Segers' new showpiece. It is no surprise to learn that Alaïa collects Newson-designed pieces and that they feature in his own three-room mini hotel, which is in the same complex of buildings on rue de Moussy.

Segers and Newson seem to be developing an interesting partnership for the creation of unusual environments. The Azzedine Alaïa store is preceded by the MHT store (the jewellery store of Marie-Hélène de Taillac) in Tokyo, completed in 2005, which uses high-gloss lacquer, leather and mirrors to create the impression of an oversized jewellery box. They also created one of the room designs for Puerta América, Madrid, the hotel which is itself a jewellery box for contemporary design.

Left and below: **Azzedine Alaïa Paris.** View of the store from the main showroom. The main feature is the 12 display cases, upholstered in calfskin, halfway up the curving wall

CUSTOM MADE

Above: Azzedine Alaïa Paris. The base of the marble pillar fans out to form a circular banquette, dressed with six calfskin cushions

Left: Azzedine Alaïa Paris. View of the store from the street, with the buildings of rue de Moussy reflected in the glass entrance doors

Above: Azzedine Alaïa Paris. Detail of one of the calfskin display cases

Below: Azzedine Alaïa Paris. Plan of the new accessories showcase, which is just 23 square metres

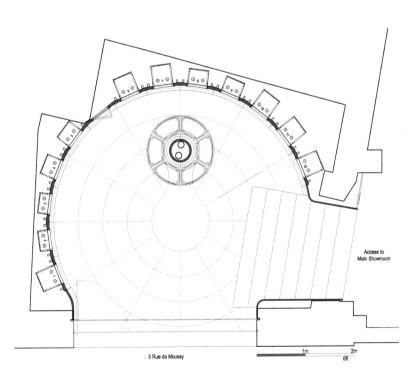

5 Rue de Moussy

Access to
Main Showroom

1m   2m

6ft

Massimiliano and
Doriana Fuksas

Emporio Armani

Hong Kong 2002

It is a surprise to see that Giorgio Armani chose the exciting Fuksas duo to design the new Emporio Armani in Hong Kong: the Armani group is typically associated with conservative cuts and clean lines, and for the Giorgio Armani stores worldwide, Armani chose the leading minimalist architect Claudio Silvestrin for his understated sophistication (see Claudio Silvestrin in Chapter 2). An 'emporium' is literally a warehouse, and the Armani emporium is certainly that – it is a vast store that sells anything from books and cosmetics to exquisite clothes and suits.

The Armani/Chater House in Hong Kong, which incorporates both the clean lines of Claudio Silvestrin for the GA line and the dynamic forms of the Fuksas collaboration, carries with it a new agenda for the Armani fashion group: to appeal to a younger and more dynamic clientele than the typical Armani loyalists.

The development is strategically sited at the junction of two busy shopping streets in downtown Hong Kong. The Emporio Armani, designed by Fuksas, refuses any form of traditional architectural formalism and develops a concept of fluidity by studying the paths of people's movement through the store. The attention is less on the objects within the space than on the space itself, whether empty or decorated.

Double walls of curved glass incised with an abstract pattern move through the spaces, from internal to external, to form the backdrop for the merchandise: the effect is to render the garments apparently weightless in this almost liquid environment. The lighting systems disappear and the glass wall becomes the source of light itself. The blue-coloured epoxy resin floor, which runs throughout the store, reflects the image of the ceiling, blurring boundaries between top and bottom. The stainless steel furniture is clad in soft and translucent materials that are comfortable to use.

The transition between spaces – from the Emporio shop, through the café, bookshop, cosmetics shop and flower shop – becomes fluid as one space disappears into another. The restaurant entertains the most thrilling detail – the red fibreglass ribbon that traces spirals in the air like the dancing ribbons of Chinese gymnasts. The red ribbon emerges, flies, and captures a wonderful sense of movement, otherwise difficult to make manifest in architecture. The intense luminosity and the colour of light in the store varies from the day to the night. The facade on Chater Road reflects the mutations of Hong Kong city with a continuously changing illuminated graphic sign.

Fuksas and Fuksas went on to design the new Emporio Armani in Shanghai.

Left and right: Emporio Armani Hong Kong. The café on the second floor. The red fibreglass ribbon emerges from the floor to become a bar table, then rises and drops to create a dining space, intersects to house a DJ stand, rises to provide a bar space, then turns to form a spiral tunnel that defines the main entrance. The spiral is 105 metres long, 70 centimetres wide and 8 centimetres thick

Below: Emporio Armani Hong Kong. The main display areas feature double walls of curved glass forming a backdrop for the merchandise

CUSTOM MADE

Above, top: **Emporio Armani Hong Kong.** The red ribbon weaves through the bar and dining area

Above, bottom: **Emporio Armani Hong Kong.** Menswear. The double glass curved wall defines the space of the store, winding its way around the garments, with black ribbons playing on this theme in the ceiling

Left: **Emporio Armani Hong Kong.** The various retail levels are connected with dramatic stainless steel staircases with glazed treads and transparent Plexiglas handrails

Left: Emporio Armani Hong Kong. In the flower shop, the vases are realised in transparent Plexiglas that gives extreme lightness to the shop area and the impression that the flowers are floating

Right: Emporio Armani Hong Kong. The exhibition walls to the right of the bookshop are in satin Plexiglas and stainless steel. The colours of the shelves alternate between red and white

Below: Emporio Armani Hong Kong. The red ribbon spirals through the entranceway

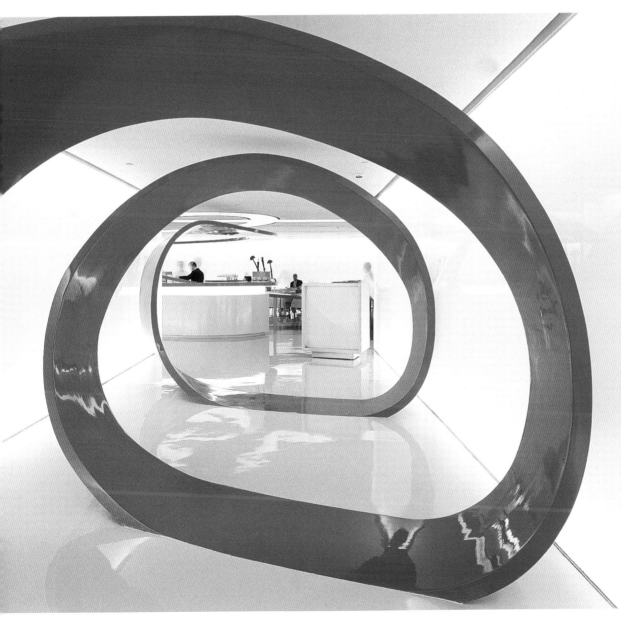

Above and opposite, top: **Emporio Armani Hong Kong.** The cosmetics store. All furniture, designed by Fuksas and Fuksas, is made of stainless steel but clad in soft translucent Plexiglas

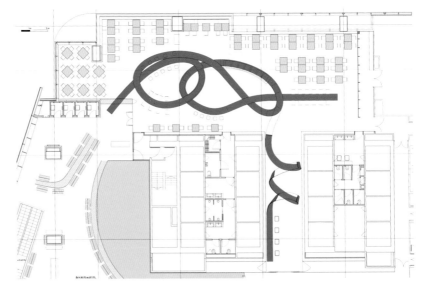

Right and far right: **Emporio Armani Hong Kong.**
Café plan and rendering

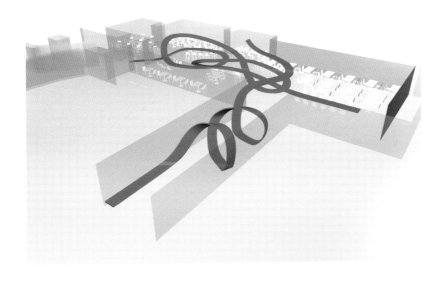

Virgile and Stone with fgs
(implementation architects, Milan)

Burberry

Milan 2003

London-based Virgile and Stone were commissioned by Burberry to create a new store that would launch the British luxury brand into Italy. Burberry is perhaps best known for its 'Britishness', a theme that it has carried through into a fashionable, iconic brand, with an edge on traditional items such as the rainproof mackintosh and the umbrella. The store in Milan is the first Burberry store in Italy. The brief was to bring to life the site, a 16th-century Milanese landmark building, by encapsulating the new and progressive spirit of Burberry.

The building extends over three floors with a double-height facade that gives an immediate view, from street level, of the scale and diversity of the store. A cantilevered nickel and glass staircase links the three floors. The design approach by Virgile and Stone is 'contemporary but drawing from the heritage of the established brand' while also including contemporary art pieces from artists all over the world. Authentic British materials have been sourced but used in an innovative way; for example, the length of the building is lined with handworked English oak sitting next to high-gloss lacquered surfaces. Bespoke cabinetwork is detailed with nickel finishing, glass and lacquer.

Above: Burberry Milan. The ground floor houses bags, perfume and other accessories. The inner courtyard is accessed from the rear of the store

The store is flooded with natural light and uses a natural palette of colours as the backdrop for each floor, but it is also rich in texture and tone. It is zoned into 'British scenes'. On the first floor a stylish lounge has been created, with a small bar and homely fireplace, offering a relaxed interlude from the stresses of shopping. Womenswear is more contemporary with a range of artistic details including the bound canes of Finnish artist Jakku Pernu, a large diptych by Dan Hays at the end of the room, and miniature, illuminated photographs of the catwalk placed above the hanging display units. The 'Men's Club' offers a personalised Burberry tailoring service with traditional cutting tables; suits and garments are displayed in heavy ornate oak cabinets with integrated leather straps and pockets to house accessories.

A 'Rainroom' has been specially created for the gabardine raincoat, one of Burberry's iconic garments. The British weather is celebrated with a 19-metre-long video installation piece projected onto the panelled ceiling.

There is an internal courtyard that is landscaped using traditional inlaid stone flooring and is the setting for a contemporary abstract sculpture created in collaboration with Jaakku Pernu – a series of interwoven canes cut from willow, reminiscent of British country hedgerows. Other collaborations include British artists McCollin Bryan's resin cast plinths that house the new Burberry Home Collection.

Right and below: **Burberry Milan.** A 'Rainroom' has been specially created for the traditional gabardine raincoat, one of Burberry's iconic garments. The British weather is celebrated with a 19-metre-long video installation piece projected onto the panelled ceiling

THE ART OF THE TRENCH

Above and opposite: Burberry Milan. Womenswear on the second level has a slightly more contemporary edge to it with a range of artistic details – from the bound canes of Finnish artist Jaakko Pernu (top left), to the miniature illuminated photographs of the catwalk placed above the hanging display units (above), a seated mannequin (far left) and a large diptych by artist Dan Hays at the far end of the room (near left)

Above: Burberry Milan. The 'Men's Club' offers a personalised Burberry tailoring service with traditional cutting tables (rear of image), and shirts are in the time honoured fashion laid out on individual shelves

Right: Burberry Milan. The first floor is designed with a stylish lounge in mind, akin to a typically 'British scene' with small bar and homely fireplace, offering a relaxed interlude from the stresses of shopping

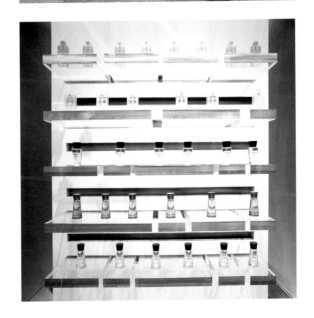

Left, top, middle and bottom: **Burberry Milan.**
Accessories and perfumes are now big business for
most fashion houses, and so too is the traditional
British umbrella, housed in its own box

Above: **Burberry Milan.** Floor plans

Sophie Hicks Architects

Paul Smith

London 1998
Milan 2001

In contrast to many of the other projects in this chapter, Sophie Hicks Architects has deliberately reflected the location of the store in the architectural design for Paul Smith. Led by Paul Smith's eclectic style, the architecture for the stores is unique to each location, mirroring the eccentricity of the fashion.

Located next to Portobello Road, famous for its busy markets and its Notting Hill celebrities, Westbourne House allowed Paul Smith, who is very cautious in committing to stand-alone shops, to fulfil his wish to display his designs in a domestic house away from a hardcore retail neighbourhood. The townhouse he chose was dilapidated so the transformation into a retail outlet first required substantial rebuilding. A central atrium was created to allow more light into the house and interior walls were stripped out, but some of the names of the rooms reveal the former home's original set-up: accessories are in The Dining Room, while The Playroom is for childrenswear. The clothes are displayed in furniture – dresses are hanging inside wardrobes – which evokes a domestic feel by being typical of a house of this style and period. Westbourne House has received two architectural awards and led to Sophie Hicks's appointment to design the Milan store.

Located in a site that architecturally typifies the city, Paul Smith Milan is set in the 18th-century Palazzo Gallarati Scotti which faces onto a busy street. The centrepiece of the store is a courtyard, surrounded by double-height rooms and galleries, along with smaller, more intimate spaces.

Despite the introduction of new interior features, such as illuminated dividing panels, care has been taken to emphasise the original detailing of the building and walls have been plastered using age-old, local Italian techniques. The terrazzo floor of the original palace has been kept, invigorating new designs for mosaic flooring and a very contemporary terrazzo stairway which is suspended from a hanging glass panel.

Antique furniture was sourced by the architects to match the palace's decaying beauty while plain glass has been used for the display cabinets and tabletops.

Both stores have highlighted Paul Smith's ability to transform traditional ideas with a heavy accent on the idiosyncratic and a contemporary twist.

Above: **Paul Smith Milan.** The double-height store gives a wonderful feeling of space and allows the vibrant pink plastered walls not to stifle the fashions. Display tables, shelves and hanging rails, in contrast, create clean and simple lines

Right: **Paul Smith Milan.** The old and the new sit side by side in this room full of colour and bathed in natural light. Ties are amusingly hung on the oversized flower, reached from the glass mezzanine level that looks down from above

Above: **Paul Smith Milan.** The original architectural features of the palazzo were retained as seen in the corridor of shelves. Paul Smith's colourful designs sit comfortably in this all-plaster, pink environment

Right: **Paul Smith Milan.** Interior view of main room, with original arched architectural features and the use of antique furniture in the foreground

Left: **Paul Smith London.** Exterior view of Westbourne House, a grand townhouse in the heart of Notting Hill

Below: **Paul Smith London.** Menswear on the ground floor where the clothes are displayed in wardrobes and chandeliers hang from the ceiling, retaining the old feel of the house

Below: **Paul Smith London.** The accessories
are displayed in a traditional cabinet with a
heavy wrought-iron chandelier hanging above.
Walls throughout the house are adorned with
pictures in all shapes and sizes

Below: **Paul Smith London.** Womenswear on the
first floor takes on a bedroom theme in whites, soft
fabrics, and comfortable chairs

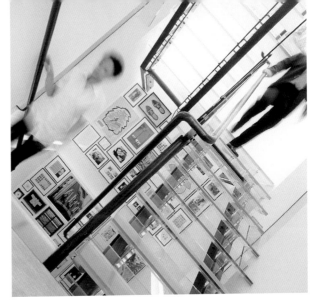

Right: **Paul Smith London.** The glass staircase injects a very contemporary edge to the centre of this grand townhouse, flooding it with natural light from above

Below: **Paul Smith London.** Display of Paul Smith suits and ties, the mainstay of the designer's label

Curiosity with lighting designed by
Gwenael Nicolas

Issey Miyake

Paris 1999
Tokyo 2000

Issey Miyake's distinctive fashion designs require a very distinctive environment within which to be displayed. Miyake's range for Pleats Please places emphasis on the most often 'crinkled' texture of the garment, as well as his famous one-seam cut. Pleats Please stores are throughout the world, and in most instances Miyake chooses different architects for each store. In this example, he commissioned Tokyo-based architects Curiosity to design both his second store in Paris on Rue des Rosiers and the store in the distinguished shopping district of Aoyama in Tokyo.

The second Pleats Please in Paris (the other is located on Boulevard St Germain) is located in a diverse, multicultural and lively neighbourhood and is housed in the converted premises of a former Turkish bath. The store is small and minimal but with colourful accents. It changes from day to night, becoming a gallery of video images after dark.

The facade is glass but with a ghostly fogging effect, and the Pleats Please signage folds in and out like a pleat. The interior space is dominated by two installations. The first of these 'retail sculptures' is a vivid honeycomb, made out of aluminium, which serves as both a display case and a storage unit. The second is a cool blue cube, made from enamelled steel, which contains the sales counter and gives access to the fitting rooms. This deep azure shade penetrates the room and is a refreshing touch to the otherwise brick and stone of Parisian streets. The result of the interior design gives this small tight space an airy and spacious ambience.

In contrast, the Pleats Please store in Aoyama, Tokyo, boasts an interior full of natural light. It is stark and, apart from a striking curtain made from neoprene that covers one wall of the shop, the only sources of colour are from Issey Miyake's fantastic garments. (The curtain's colour changes according to season.)

The store has silver-grey flooring on the ground level and a silvery-grey ceiling on the first floor, encapsulating the entire space in a silvery shell. Transparent tables and stools in varying heights, made from stainless steel and acrylic, act as display units for accessories, leaving all emphasis to be placed on Miyake's designs. On entering the store the client is confronted with the stairs to the upper floor or a 'bridge' to another section – designed to give clients views of garments from different angles and encourage them to explore.

Above: **Pleats Please Paris.** The facade is glass but with a ghostly fogging effect with the Pleats Please signage folding in and out like a pleat. Miyake's designs stand out even from the street as the only colour and distinct objects in view

Right: **Pleats Please Paris.** The honeycomb installation, made from aluminium, acts as both display case and storage unit. An amusing and innovative solution for retail display

Above left and right: **Pleats Please Paris.** Views of the cool blue cube. Fitting rooms are also accessed from this area, as well as the concealed counter. This use of 360 degrees of blue gives the otherwise small store a feeling of spaciousness

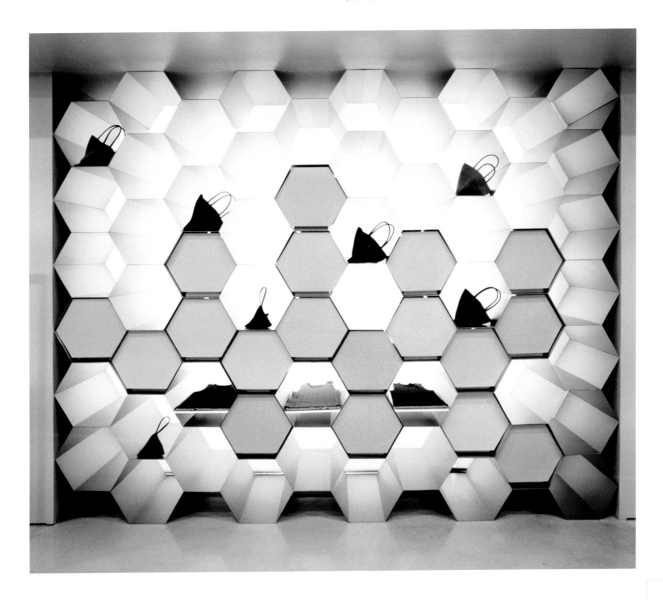

Right: **Pleats Please Tokyo.** Garments and accessories compose the space with their distinct colours, like sculptures in a translucent and steel-edged room

Left: **Pleats Please Tokyo.** The first floor continues with the theme of the curtain and directs all attention to the garments, which are sparsely hung on the minimal stainless steel rails

Above: **Pleats Please Tokyo.** Detail of the transparent acrylic accessory tables on wheels. The table is almost invisible suggesting that the accessories are floating in the store

Below: **Pleats Please Tokyo.** Detail of standing tables and stools made from steel

Cho Slade Architecture
with GaA Architects

Martine Sitbon

Seoul 2002

Commissioned to provide a Seoul home for the fashions of French designer Martine Sitbon, Cho Slade of New York, with local architects GaA Architects, crafted a jewellery box out of a former townhouse in the Cheongdam-dong shopping district. Both classic and modern, the fashions of Martine Sitbon change from season to season, a characteristic that the architects considered when designing the 'timeless' space that would host the collections. The half-buried commercial area at the base of the house was originally the garage and storage areas, with ceiling heights ranging from 1.75 metres to 6 metres. Cho Slade exploited this restrictive characteristic of the building by wrapping the entire interior volume in a continuous surface that bends around corners, floors and ceiling.

Above **Martine Sitbon Seoul.** The far end of the glass facade offers a preview of the store as well as reflecting the neighbourhood's urban fabric

The exterior is a glass skin made up of two rows 12.5 metres wide by 3.6 metres tall, stacked on top of one another to create a glass wall at the end of the building. During the day the top row of glass reflects the blue of the sky, while the ground-floor row offers a transparent view into the store. At night, the building transforms into a mirrored wall that, rather than reflecting the surrounding neighbourhood, reveals the strong solidity of a wall with its rough polyester paint.

Clothes are displayed using objects in the space: suspended, they appear to float or are subject to the tensions of the architectural dynamics that seamlessly connect the varying heights of the ceiling. The weightlessness is enhanced by the backdrop of a uniform surface compound that literally wraps the floor, walls and ceiling. Whilst glass is the store's outer skin, a buttery-yellow glistening skin envelopes the interior. This glossy finish could give a 'flashy' feel to the store, but is played down due to its neutral tone and the contemporary nature of the display.

The verticality of the movable display racks exaggerates the tightness of the space. The warped surface of the front side of the racks implies a liquid shaped by surface tension, while the mirrored backs, together with the glass shelf and dressing-room mirror, provide a sharp-edged counterpoint to the rounded edges of the space.

The sales counter is made of soft silicone whose smooth edges welcome both client and salesperson. The finish looks much the same as the walls and floor, but in contrast is soft and squishy.

Above and right: **Martine Sitbon Seoul.** Dawn
through to dusk, the store's glass skin changes to
accommodate the differing reflections of each time
of day – from blue sky to the towers of adjacent
buildings

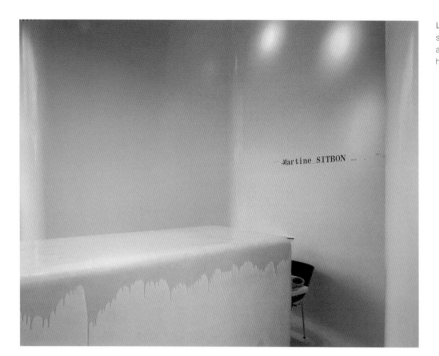

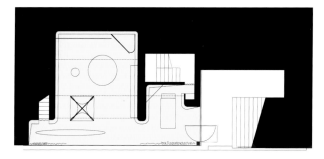

Above: **Martine Sitbon Seoul.** Plan

Below: **Martine Sitbon Seoul.** A wide view of the interior of the store, with the black polished oversized pebble dominating the floor space

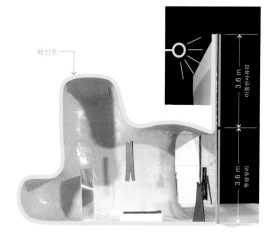

페인트

3.6 m 이중반사유리

3.6 m 투명유리

Above: **Martine Sitbon Seoul.** Concept plan

Above: **Martine Sitbon Seoul.** Garments are suspended and float in the space, whilst interrupted by the sharp edges of the mirrored screen. The cocoon-like linear object that floats behind the facade accentuates the length of the space and the symmetry between floor and ceiling

Above: **Martine Sitbon Seoul.** Daytime view of the entrance and facade

Above: **Martine Sitbon Seoul.** The store at night almost glows, with a rusted golden hue to the upper floor

Right: **Martine Sitbon Seoul.** The length of the transparent facade at night, with the soft silicone cash desk between two dressed mannequins in the foreground

6a Architects
with Tom Emerson

Oki-ni

London 2001

The distinctive architectural treatment of Oki-ni expresses a departure from a usual retail concept – it's a 'shopfront' for clothes that are only available online from the Oki-ni website. So why have a store if the actual act of the sale happens in cyberspace and not real space?

Oki-ni is offering the fashion market a new relationship between client and product: limited edition clothes and accessories by well-known brands, such as Oki-ni/Adidas Handball Special trainers, are available only via the Internet from Oki-ni. However, fashion is a tactile business, and the total experience of the 'shop' has always been more than just a point of sale.

6a Architects won the commission to design this store (and the concessions that followed) with an installation-based concept that emphasises the tactile and social opportunities of clothes in the shopping environment. The three large windows which make up its facade reveal a felt landscape contained by an oak 'tray' inserted into the existing concrete shell. The steep upward sides of the fan-shaped tray divide the main shop from the changing room but primarily serve as an oddly domestic hanging rail for clothes. The walls that are visible above the tray's sides are made of rough, unfinished concrete that provides a contrast of textures.

There is no traditional shelving. Apart from on the tray walls, the other displays are laid out on top of large, rectangular piles of felt, which can also be used as furniture, and hollow metal lengths. The hollows provide space for a low-level library of books about design, art and photography.

With all transactions conducted online, the point of sale is missing, and so too are the cash desks. 6a have avoided any obvious concentration of technology and a laptop provides the sales interface. This is meant to be casually placed amongst the products and visitors, but in truth, it is usually set in front of a shop assistant, standing at what could be mistaken for a lectern. 6a Architects has won major awards for the design of Oki-ni, but are we ready for it? The assistants have to explain the concept to first-time shoppers, while it seems unlikely that many people really are going to make room amongst the diplays so they can lounge about and read a book.

It is interesting that the London store is situated on Savile Row, a street famous the world over for traditional men's tailoring. With its limited editions, Oki-ni is leaning towards a bespoke service and its heavy use of wood can be seen as derivative of the conventional wood panelling of establishment tailors. Its position at the north end of the street also places it within the immediate vicinity of the design, new media and film companies whose employees are most likely to feel at home in this retail adventure.

Above: **Oki-ni London.** The store, seen from Savile Row, has three large windows that give it a very expansive, open image

Right and below: **Oki-ni London.** The large piles of felt act as both display units and furniture. Explicit lighting, using low-hung bare bulbs, gives the store its studio feel

Above: **Oki-ni London.** Clothes hang from the low sides of the oak tray in a casual domestic way, as though in one's own bedroom

Above: **Oki-ni London.** Concept sketch of clients using the felt piles as furniture whilst they also function as display tables

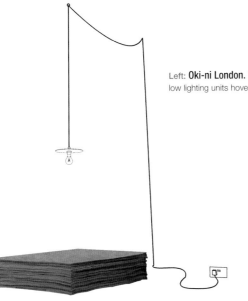

Left: **Oki-ni London.** Detail of the casual and low lighting units hovering above the felt piles

Above: **Oki-ni London.** Model of the oak tray that has been inserted into the store space

Above: **Oki-ni London.** The laptop is the only reference to technology in the store, and acts as a sales interface, but not the sale itself. It is casually placed on the felt pile for both clients and store assistants to use

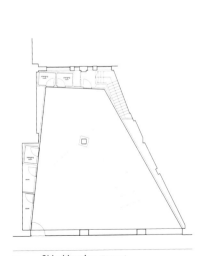

Above: **Oki-ni London.** Plan of store

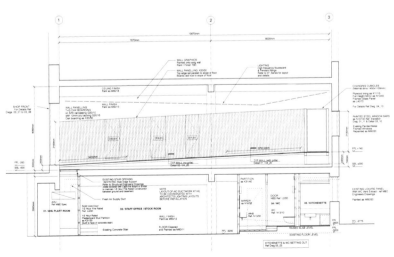

Above: **Oki-ni London.** Section of store

Gabellini Associates
with Gianfranco Ferré

Gianfranco Ferré Boutique and Spa
Milan 2003

Gianfranco Ferré's fashion designs are known for their weight – in luxury, in presence, in fabrics, and in design. It is an international name but very much rooted in Italy. Gianfranco Ferré himself first trained as an architect before turning his talents to fashion design, and now produces lines for both mens- and womenswear. Seen as a collaboration, Gabellini Associates (based in New York) initiated the basic architectural concepts for this prominent store in the heart of Milan, and Gianfranco Ferré himself completed the details and gave it the finishing touches.

Not only is this boutique remarkable in its real estate – the store spans across an archway on the second floor of a period building that leads to a Zen-like courtyard – but it is also the first of its kind to also house a spa. Shopping and spas have finally found each other! It is not obvious what the connections are between high fashion and spas, other than that both are luxurious, but the dominating factor behind this specific union is that they are owned by the same parent company – IT Holdings. The spa is opulent and, despite being in a tight urban setting, looks out onto the green and pebbled courtyard at the back of the building.

The store itself is spread across two levels and lies symmetrically either side of the front-entrance archway, with menswear to the left and womenswear to the right (with a hallway linking the store from womenswear to the Ferré Spa). The various spaces are defined by distinct interior elements and connected through the continuity of textures, shapes and lines. In addition, the use of folding panels and mobile screens gives each area its own flexibility.

The spaces are luxurious and no expense has been spared in the choice of materials and attention to detail. The backdrop is dominated by red, mostly in panels, giving the store its intimate and sensuous edge, and the abundant use of dark woods adds to the richness of the environment. Accessory cases are made from rare woods – zebrano and mahogany – and given a gloss-finish to show off the grain. The sofas are covered with precious leathers while the trays are patterned with mother-of-pearl mosaics. The walls of the men's area feature leather panelling, whilst silk is used for womenswear. Beige and red tones are found dotted throughout the store and a soft pink hue sets the ground-floor women's section unmistakably apart from the rest.

Above: Gianfranco Ferré Milan. The stairway, in red resin glass with carpeted steel chrome steps, leads up to womenswear on the first floor

Above: Gianfranco Ferré Milan. The accessories area features mica screens and luxurious cabinets. Precious leather pouches and open trunks house other accessories in the background

Above, below and right: **Gianfranco Ferré Milan**.
View through to menswear at the back of the store,
that overlooks the courtyard. The wall of the rear
section is panelled with red leather

Gabellini Associates

Nicole Farhi

New York 1999

The Nicole Farhi store in New York is a prime example of where fashion retail has extended beyond itself into other areas of business which, hopefully, still enhance the brand. In this case, fashion merges with fine dining and the brand has also lent itself to a homeware range. Whilst still very much a store dedicated to Nicole Farhi's collection of elegant fashions in typically refined textiles, the 1999 venture was significant in pushing the boundaries of what fashion symbolises today. Michael Gabellini, known for his minimalist interior architecture that utilises touches of sensuality, was the perfect match for Farhi.

The New York store occupies a 1901 landmark building which was formerly home to the famous Copacabana nightclub. The exterior of the Beaux-Arts building was restored with Indiana limestone and Deer Isle granite in order to complement the original stone. The entrance to the store brings the customer across a glass bridge that runs between two double-height atria and leads into womenswear, which effectively hovers over the basement restaurant. This 'floating platform' is comprised of American walnut and honed New York bluestone floors. The latter visually connects the floor to the blue-plaster ceiling of the restaurant below.

Two staircases lead down from womenswear, one directly into the restaurant and the other to the home and menswear collections. From this level, there is another entrance to the restaurant via floating wooden steps. The overall effect of the bridge and atria is to give due prominence to the restaurant, even though it's in the basement. 4,000 square feet – over one third of the retail space – is given over to the dining area, which has significant architectural features including a 30-foot-long luminescent bar-table and a seemingly floating glass cube that houses the open kitchen.

Farhi was far better known in London than in New York when she opened this two-pronged venture, but this retail and restaurant synthesis has proven to be successful.

Above: **Nicole Farhi New York.** The 1901 landmark building at night

Right: **Nicole Farhi New York.** The 4,000-square-foot restaurant is marked by a 30-foot-long luminescent bar-table, but the main focus is the water-white glass cube floating on a raised bluestone plinth that houses the open kitchen

New Departments

Department stores, with their large floorprints and variety of components, may offer a wide scope for designers, but they are undoubtedly a double-edged sword. Many of the older buildings that require internal reinvention are grand and classical, but they are also tremendously restrictive. Designers often have to follow set grids and deal with immovable escalators, stairs, fire exits and service areas. Each floor may be a huge expanse, unbroken by anything of existing architectural interest and beleaguered by low, modular ceilings, or else, in a more upright building, the designer is faced with an incomprehensible warren of rooms. Worse still, the designers have to weigh up how to balance the 'brand' of the stores against the myriad of concessions, and when designing several floors need to force consistent elements to work within the context of different product-types. To cap it all, in terms of rate per square metre, revenue is unlikely to match that available for a boutique. Yet there is a growing raft of designers who have picked their way through this minefield to offer admirable and sometimes astonishing solutions.

That boutiques have led the fashion retail revolution is no accident. The fashion designer is likely to be a creative person who values identity,

New Departments

innovation and style: the space is small and the concepts can be high. After all, the word 'boutique' conjures a sense of the individual, bespoke environment, and this matches the increasing personalisation of lifestyle culture. Design-savvy customers want 'something different'. Within the boutique, the architectural designer and the fashion designer can work together to offer just that. By contrast, department store design in the mid- to late 20th century was dominated by the lowest common denominator. It is extremely hard for designers to convey the necessity of high concepts to a department store's boardroom of people who are only intent on shifting the highest number of units to the masses. However, the radical American designer Jordan Mozer managed to do just that to the owners of Karstadt, the uninspiring middle-market chain, by presenting a slide show which opened with: 'Hellomynameisjordanmozerandiampleasedtohavethisopportunitytomeetyou anddiscussthedesignofyourstoresiamtroubledbythelackofpunctuationinthest oresthereremanydifferentproductsandmanydifferenttypesofcustomers…'

Karstadt got the message, as have an increasing number of department stores within the last few years. Although they may be huge and have a multi-retail purpose, department stores can still access the burgeoning luxury market if they offer a sense of the bespoke within a characterful and well-orientated space. The resultant, distinctive design can also be used to extenuate the quality and individuality of the store's brand, preventing it from being subsumed by the maze of concessions. In theory, this does not sound like rocket science – the principles are straightforward – but it can take a long time for an elephant to turn around.

Fortunately, absorbing the principles of how architectural design and retail can work together has led to a variety of solutions with different stresses. When the first edition of *Fashion Retail* was published in 2004, it seemed that department stores were best able to incorporate the more radical principles of high design by starting from scratch. In the UK, London-based stores such as Selfridges and Harvey Nichols sought out space in the regions where it was still possible to secure enough property for a major new development in a town centre. The Birmingham Selfridges project remains a model of how the mundane mammoth of a genre can be reworked to tremendous effect, and the building has become a major architectural icon. However, with hindsight, this was not to be the beginnings of a reinvention of department store culture worldwide. It proved to be something of a minor epoch, largely limited to the UK. Surprisingly, the last few years have shown that it is inside the older buildings where the renaissance is still gathering momentum, and this is a worldwide phenomenon.

This chapter charts how designers have managed to work around the pitfalls of existing spaces to offer a new dynamism to the sector. All of the designers have brought elements of successful boutique design into the department store, allowing a feeling of individuality and luxury to permeate the design through the use of texture, pattern and form in a way that surprises and delights. Part of the key has been to realise the importance of detail and variation when working on a grand scale.

To different degrees, the designs involve an experiential rolling narrative that leads to one focal point or a series of distinct interventions – this is the opposite of the disorientating repetition that previously seemed to define department store design. Rather than feeling lost in an endless, flickering blaze of white neon, the customer becomes part of an unusual, suggestive and textured story that holds within it personal associations and cross-cultural connections. The layers and breadth of the space enhance the thoroughness and depth of the narrative.

Furthermore, designers have used the fact that department stores, by their very nature, house disparate styles and objects to develop a sense of the curated space in the manner of the most progressive galleries and museums. Perhaps inspired by the way that style magazine design has developed, designers and retail managers can create focal points, free of the constraints of concession or boutique regimentation, that allow for an intelligent merging – or collision – of disparate items or styles. If done well, this should not come across as just hackneyed juxtaposition, but the layering of a story with matter from different sources. It creates a new adventure that a boutique, usually purveying just one strand of luxury, cannot hope to mirror. This lies at the heart of the success of both Universal Design Studio's designs for Lotte in Seoul and Rei Kawakubo's Dover Street Market. Offering a series of cultural and spatial 'accidents', the latter toys with convention so much that customers do not even realise that it is a department store. Through these expansive approaches, department stores are finally beginning to fulfil their potential as crucibles of adventure, rather than institutions of dour convenience.

Future Systems

Selfridges

Birmingham 2003

Birmingham has undergone a massive central redevelopment in recent years, which has included a new canalside cultural quarter, a greater focus on the arts and the introduction of upmarket retail ventures such as the Mailbox. With the success of Selfridges Manchester, Vittorio Radice decided to continue the department store's expansion beyond its famous central London Oxford Street store with an architectural landmark for the UK's second largest city.

This was a bold stroke and required a bold architectural partner: Future Systems, who also worked with Radice on radical designs for the Manchester branch's food hall. Its design for the exterior of the Birmingham store was to be another leap forward. Stemming from a Paco Rabanne dress and other more organic natural forms, the result was a departure from any other department store to date. Selfridges Birmingham opened in September 2003 and has been a huge success for Selfridges, Future Systems and Birmingham itself.

Situated in Birmingham's 'Bull Ring', the site offered a pretty mixed backdrop of red brick, modern retail and grey ringroads. The Bull Ring is the site of the traditional marketplace and this has been continued in its new development in the form of a mixed retail mall. Directly opposite the site is St Martin's Church, a Victorian neo-Gothic church that is perhaps the only historic building in the site's immedite vicinity.

Working within this context, Future Systems' architecture provides a strikingly alternative backdrop for St Martin's angular and vertical neo-Gothic style. The building's form makes reference to the fall of fabric, and its skin curves around the inner shell like the soft lines of a body; there is no distinction between walls and roof, and no angles that break this organic flow of fabric. It is one continuous movement of architecture and interrupts the city's environment with its horizon of a scaly blue wave.

Inspired by the sequins on the 1960s Paco Rabanne dress, and the movement of the 'chain-dress', also by Paco Rabanne, the exterior of the building is enveloped in a skin made up of 16,000 aluminium discs, creating a lustrous grain. The pattern is constant, like that of a fly's eye, and follows the rhythms of the curves as discs are placed slightly closer together or further apart. In bright sunlight, the discs shimmer, and similarly reflect the changing weather conditions. Combined with its aluminium wave of a 'skirting board' that lines the bottom of the building, the structure takes on the colours and shapes of the people or things that pass by. It creates a most distinct surface area that literally glows amongst the skyline of its neighbouring buildings. The surface onto which the discs are attached is

Above: **Selfridges Birmingham.** The wave (right) was inspired by the sequins on the 1960s Paco Rabanne dress (top), and the movement of the 'chain-dress' (above) also by Paco Rabanne. The exterior of the building is enveloped in a skin made up of 16,000 aluminium discs, creating a lustrous grain

painted a deep 'Yves Klein' blue, and is flooded with blue light at night – allowing the discs to sit in shadow and the blue background to glow.

The lid of the building has a free-form opening that pours down light into a great atrium, permitting a clear view of the sky from within and giving a very real sense of the weather conditions outside. Large, sinuously shaped openings carved from the form offer themselves as display windows and are the only view out of the store other than the upward reaching skylight.

The four-storey building has four entrances on three different levels, one of which is from a spectacular 17-metre-high pedestrian bridge leading from the multistorey car park.

The key to Future Systems' interior is the deep atrium, criss-crossed by a white-clad cat's cradle of escalators that holds the floors together, whilst also setting up a play on textures – the handrails are made from glossy fibreglass, while the undersides of the escalators are clad in matt plaster.

As with the Manchester store, different designers were commissioned to create the interior, resulting in four very distinct retail areas. Future Systems designed Level 1 which includes the food hall and other levels were designed by Eldridge Williams, Stanton Williams and Cibic Partners/Lees Associates.

Below: **Selfridges Birmingham.** Twilight. The outstanding building creates the most distinct surface area that literally glows amongst the skyline of its neighbouring structures

Above: Selfridges Birmingham. The four-storey building has four entrances on three different levels, one of which is from a spectacular 17-metre-high pedestrian bridge leading from the multistorey car park

Above and right: Selfridges Birmingham. The interior of the building is a deep atrium, criss-crossed by a white-clad 'cat's cradle' of escalators that holds the floors together

Above: **Selfridges Birmingham.** The surface to which the discs are attached is painted a deep 'Yves Klein' blue, and is flooded with blue light at night – allowing the discs to sit in shadow and the blue background to glow

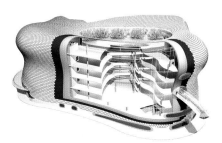

Selfridges Birmingham. Cut away

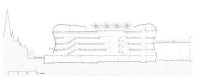

Selfridges Birmingham. Section

Selfridges Birmingham. Site plan

Universal Design Studio

Lotte

Seoul 2005–7

Following the acclaim of the Stella McCartney store designs, London-based Universal Design Studio was approached by Lotte to help redesign the interiors of its five-storey department store in the Myeongdong district of Seoul, South Korea. At the same time as understanding that a modern-day, upmarket department store must compete with boutiques while offering its own cohesive, curated and branded experience, Universal addressed one of the major problems that have long compromised department store interiors: how to explore the drama of a large space while resisting the visual monotony that beleaguers the genre and makes it the poor cousin of fashion retail design.

The collaboration with Lotte began in 2005 with the commission to redesign just half of the 1,000-square-metre fifth floor, but Universal's success in introducing a type of retail experience quite foreign to Korean fashionistas has led to the redesign of the third floor as well, completed in winter 2006, followed by the second half of the fifth floor, where a café/restaurant area is being introduced, due for completion in spring 2007.

Fashion retail in Seoul is very brand led and, previously, Lotte had followed the established template of dividing the department store into brand-orientated boxes. The operations of Lotte are so diverse – it is as famous for its mineral water as it is for selling clothes – that it is virtually a 'non-brand': in contrast to Virgin, it successfully traverses genres by stepping back from a forceful, cross-sector identity. Consequently, the department store had little identity beyond the franchises it housed and this suited the local retail mindset: wealthy Seoul shoppers expect branded boutiques rather than a desegregated, multi-brand experience where they can graze. Unusually, in an era where the motivation of much high-profile retail design is to create individual pockets of experience as a reaction against the homogenous whole, Universal Design Studio needed to break down the barriers and extend some idea of homogeneity into the fifth floor, creating a 'Lotte experience' beyond the women's luxury labels.

Jonathan Clarke, Director of Universal Design Studio, infused the concept with his preference for 'a space that was much more about curation', whereby an overarching intelligence actively places potentially diverse objects together to create a unique, layered environment. This approach was blended with Lotte's own desire for a design that combined 'elegance' and 'garden', which the firm called 'Eliden', a rather clunky composite of the two words.

Part of Universal's success is based on its creation of textured space through the use of pattern in a variety of materials and scales. This has been

Above: Lotte Seoul. A sculptured wall, made up of individual marquetry tiles, runs along the length of the 50-metre gallery space to create a sense of cohesion

used to great effect in smaller retail spaces, but the breadth of the Lotte project allowed the idea to be taken further. The individual concession boxes were cleared out and replaced by three distinct areas, which nonetheless remain visually connected within a 50-metre-long gallery. The same, irregular criss-cross pattern emerges in a series of screens in different materials that delineate the three areas: fret-cut, black-lacquered timber, screenprinted glass and fabric. Combining transparency and separation through the use of screens obviously draws upon Oriental design and also satisfies a local cultural leaning towards physical privacy.

Adding to the overall cohesiveness is a timber floor and, running the entire length of the gallery, a wall of three-dimensional marquetry tiles, similar to those used in the McCartney design but here drawing upon the traditional Korean interest in textiles and pattern making. Display systems include perforated sheets of vertical glass (with the clothes hangers inserted into the holes), suspended rails and clear glass units.

Meanwhile, for the third-floor accessories department, again the rabbit warren of concessions has been cleared out to create a dynamic, central space. Clarke used the privacy of screens once more, as 'accessories are highly personal', while also lending the space a feeling of transparency. The screens and the displays become one within floor-to-ceiling glass cases, inserted with underlit metal shelves. However, the most striking aspect of the display system is a series of low-level, triangular Corian units that can be placed together in different formations. The Corian surfaces are tilted to display shoes at an angle, and Clarke says this is a response to the fact that shoes are rarely displayed in the way that we usually see them. The triangular units pick up on the hard geometry of the design: regimented triangles also form the pattern of the flooring, the black Plexiglas ceiling and the screens. The masculinity is softened, though, by the shadow-pattern of dappled leaves (inspired by the stained impression of leaves on pavements) visible through the top layer of Corian. Initially, further moderation was to be provided by columns clad in living moss, but this idea proved unworkable, giving way to a live green marble.

On both floors, Universal has managed to create a balance between the identity of the store and the brands, using pattern and texture to offer a sense of event while also bringing a refreshing intelligence to product display.

Above: Lotte Seoul. The sculptured wall becomes an interesting textural backdrop to the display systems

Above and below: **Lotte Seoul.** The screen-printed glass 'room' in the fifth-floor gallery, playing on the design's theme of mixing transparency and privacy

Above: **Lotte Seoul.** The irregular, criss-cross
pattern re-emerges in another of the central rooms,
but this time is portrayed in the weightier material of
black-lacquered timber

Opposite: **Lotte Seoul.** Vertical sheets of glass are
used to create a hanging system that adds to the
theme of transparency

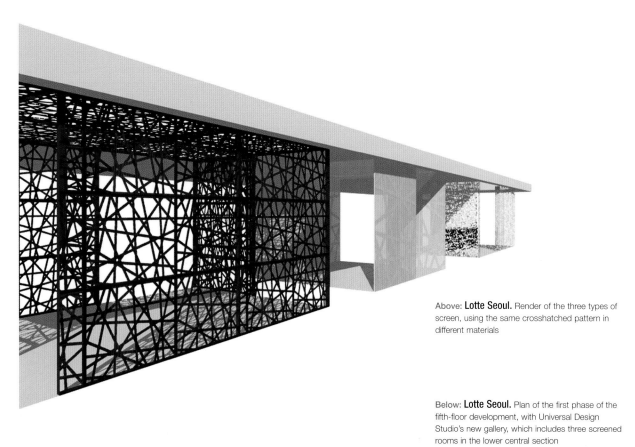

Above: Lotte Seoul. Render of the three types of screen, using the same crosshatched pattern in different materials

Below: Lotte Seoul. Plan of the first phase of the fifth-floor development, with Universal Design Studio's new gallery, which includes three screened rooms in the lower central section

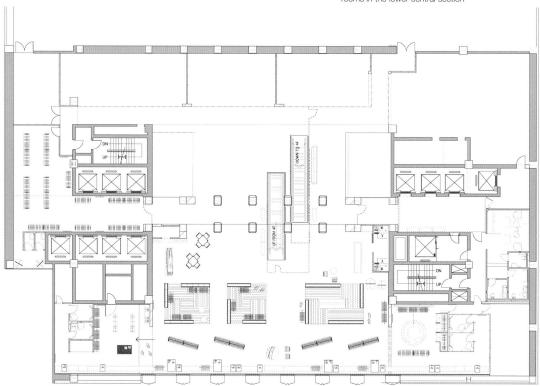

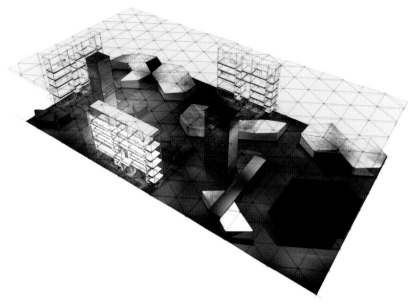

This page: **Lotte Seoul.** The design of the luxury accessories section on the third floor, completed in winter 2006, is highly geometric, with almost all elements based on a triangular form. The Corian shoe displays tilt up towards the customer

Plajer & Franz Studio

Galaxie Lafayette

Berlin 2005

In design terms, Galeries Lafayette in Berlin is one of the best-known department stores in the world. Designed by Jean Nouvel in 1995, the interior concept is based on two huge cones, both made of glass, with one rising up from ground level and the other pointing down from the top floors. The design was an assault on the conventions of linearity that had always dominated department store design, and created a circular orientation that not only looked dramatic, but also helped direct customers from floor to floor. Creating a new department within this design landmark was always going to require special consideration.

The French owners chose locally based firm Plajer & Franz to undertake the creation of Galaxie Lafayette, a 502-square-metre 'accessible luxury' area specialising in multi-branded jeanswear for girls and young women. Suitably, Plajer & Franz have formed a reputation in what can be described as the lifestyle sector of design. They have a sustained retail design relationship with both Timberland and s.Oliver, while their Universum Lounge is one of the most famous style bars in Berlin. They have also helped introduce the 'BMW lifestyle' brand to the Far East and worked with Samsung in a retail capacity.

Plajer & Franz needed to work within the established grid of the structure and also had to incorporate the tip of the descending cone, which breaks into the Galaxie Lafayette level from above. Wisely, they chose to create a design that would be sympathetic to Nouvel's conical interior architecture, while not merely repeating its themes. They also managed to create a specifically urban and chic interior that would both stand out in terms of identification and appeal to the target audience. In fact, the cone tip became the central focus of the new design, although it has not been treated with aspic reverence.

Situated almost in the middle of the space, the cone is reinvented as the centrepiece for two overlapping, large circular white ceiling discs, made of Barrisol, which could be interpreted as displaced sections of the wider upper cone. The discs set out a concept of movement and rotation that is picked up by a multi-branded display below, made up of a swirl of multilayered discs and disc perimeters. A DJ booth is incorporated into this central section, and the rims of the lower discs are LED-animated to pronounce the beat of the music with light variations. The coloured LED lights also have been inserted within Nouvel's glass cone. The synthesis of old and new elements is extenuated by a series of glass rods that surround the cone as well as falling in groups among the circular displays. The result is a dynamic gathering point for casual browsing, with a sense of the galactic furthered by the glittering black synthetic flooring and matte black ceilings surrounding the central, all-white commotion.

Above: Galaxie Lafayette Berlin. The entranceway to Galaxie Lafayette, housed within Galeries Lafayette, establishes the theme of circles and motion, coupled with a space-age edge

To one side of this central display, the circular theme emerges in one of the concept's other unusual highlights. The four dressing rooms are contained within a white cylinder with blurred images of girls punctuating its semi-transparent, double-layered plexi skin. Circles and motion also dominate the entrance to the floor. The stairs that lead into Galaxie Lafayette comprise seven more white discs, rising towards a circular ceiling recess adorned with another Barrisol disc. More translucent rods adorn the sides of the entranceway.

Apart from the multi-branded, central event space, Plajer & Franz were required to consider the needs of 15 brands with designated areas. They designed a precise yet flexible wall system that gave room for brand individuality but restricted the possibility of dominating either the overall design or neighbouring concessions. Galaxie Lafayette may be a jeanswear emporium, but Plajer & Franz have approached every aspect of the space, its freedoms and restrictions, with high-concept solutions for fashion retail.

Above and right: Galaxie Lafayette Berlin.
A matte-black ceiling and sparkling black floor lead
to the gleaming white hub of the store, a multi-
brand display area made up of LED-lit display discs
and Barrisol ceiling discs

Left and below: **Galaxie Lafayette Berlin.** The interior of Jean Nouvel's Galeries Lafayette has two glass cones which break through the levels, one pointing up from the bottom, and one pointing down from the top. The tip of the downward cone bursts through the ceiling of the new Galaxie Lafayette floor. Designers Plajer & Franz Studio decided to make it the fulcrum of their new design, with a series of discs spinning off from it

Opposite: **Galaxie Lafayette Berlin.** The four changing rooms are housed within a white cylinder. The semi-translucent plexi skin is decorated with blurred shadow images of young women

Below and right: **Galaxie Lafayette Berlin.** The 15 branded concessions around the perimeter of the floor use the same modular wall system, designed by Plajer & Franz Studio, which comprises black panels with dotted white circles and white panels with anthracite dots, ensuring that the branding of the concessions does not overpower the Galaxie theme

Above and opposite: **Galaxie Lafayette Berlin.**
The circular discs around the central cone are used
to display a sweep of garments. The white flooring
is LG Hi-Macs acrylic

left: **Galaxie Lafayette Berlin.** Plan

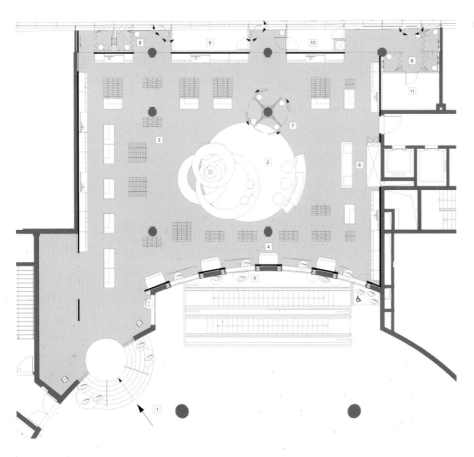

Jordan Mozer and Associates

Karstadt

Mülheim, Germany, 2003

Karstadt, one of Europe's major retailers, sought to move towards a more contemporary shopping experience for its 46,452-square-metre department store in Mülheim, outside Düsseldorf. Department stores are the unwieldly monoliths of retail design, and the Karstadt store was typical of the genre. Chicago architect and designer Jordan Mozer was hired to break it free of the sort of impersonal, repetitive and confusing layout that shoppers find increasingly unacceptable, even when balanced against the convenience of being able to shop for so many different items in one covered space. Mozer is one of the US's leading restaurant designers, but his early career involved a partnership with George Lucas of *Star Wars* fame in which they sought a way to deconstruct the shopping mall and reassemble it as an entertaining and engaging experience. That project was hit by retail recession, but the Karstadt 'lifestyle prototype' enterprise gave Mozer the opportunity to reinvigorate his ideas about retail.

Mozer's designs often border on the surreal and futuristic, but his success is rooted in his ability to reinvent historical associations within his radicalism. Surprisingly for a firm whose designs often make an outlandish visual impact, the core of each design is established by a very detailed understanding of the function of a space and how people interact with it. The plan for Karstadt Mülheim was developed after studying traditional markets in Madrid, Marrakech and Kathmandu, established high-fashion shopping streets such as London's Bond Street and Chicago's Oak Street, and the chic interiors of the likes of Jil Sander's stores.

To break up the three-storey building, the store was split into 42 zones, running along the lines of shopping streets, often with rounded focal points. The facades of the zones were deliberately small in an attempt to mirror the on-street experience, while the distinction between departments was enhanced by the use of different materials, wall, ceiling and flooring designs, and colours. The lighting is particularly effective, both through the unusual fittings that help mark out a distinct area, and through the luminescence levels – like an on-street shopping experience, there is a variance between the lighting on the 'street' and in the 'store'. Cohesiveness has been maintained within the overall design, particularly through a leaning towards the variations of rounded forms that are distinctive of Mozer designs, coupled with warm colours and a 'soft' 1970s-style geometry.

One of the major principles running through the work of Mozer and Associates is to surprise, but never threaten. The monolith may have been carved into many distinctive 'shops', but the fear of high-class boutiques,

Above and below: **Karstadt Mülheim.** Slanting doorways, jellyfish lights and curvaceous display units, all bespoke-designed by Jordan Mozer and Associates, add to the slightly surreal space theme

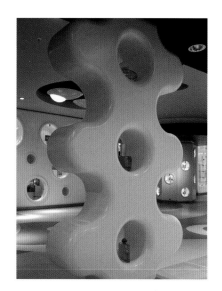

Above: Karstadt Mülheim. Jordan Mozer and Associates' overhaul pared down the floor space into individually designed zones, drawing away from the monotony and homogeneity of traditional department store design while introducing warm materials and a welcoming curvaceousness

with their sometimes forbidding facades, has been broken down by using transparency and open display systems within the facades. The round forms of the fittings help to carry the comfort/shock balance equation further. One circular junction has cone pendant lights dropping from larger inverted cones, which in turn hang from circular ceiling recesses. Another space features spiky domes and padded walls, while the electronics area has lights that look like a jellyfish with stunted entrails. On the two upper storeys, the curved motif has been carried through to the shape of the routeways.

Mozer's design is based on an understanding that diversity can no longer be matched with a one-size-fits-all, homogenous mentality. In these times of heightened lifestyle expectations, the department store has to respond by offering pockets of experience that match the shopper ID. Further, it has to offer experiential benefits beyond shopping. Karstadt's decision to break away from a reliance on its own branded products and invite designer franchises onto the premises gave Mozer the opportunity to try to create the idea of the store as a more stylish and multipurpose destination. He created a lounge bar right within the fashion section of the store to further the idea of department-store shopping as entertainment rather than chore-fuelled drudgery. Called Himmelreich, which means 'heaven', the rounded geometry of the rest of the store has here been taken further, with curved, cut-out sections in the walls allied to large, patterned cube lights and a geometric carpet. Space-age retro and cocktail cool, the bar exemplifies how far Mozer has managed to push a formerly stodgy, unadventurous store towards the lifestyle renaissance.

Above and right: Karstadt Mülheim. The entranceways to the individual zones are broken down to boutique size, with a seemingly infinite variety of materials, colours and textures used to distinguish between the individual shops. The internal 'facades' give the impression of shop windows and are used as part of the product display

Right and below: **Karstadt Mülheim.** The displays of the women's fashion area draw from the soft geometry of the floor pattern, while the men's area has a harsher linearity

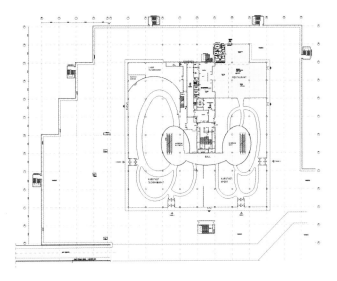

Above: **Karstadt Mülheim.** Second-floor plan

Opposite and above: **Karstadt Mülheim.** The Himmelreich café, a retro-futuristic lounge bar designed to coincide with Karstadt's attempts to shelve its fusty image and appeal to the fashion-savvy

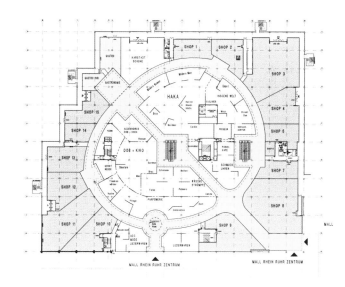

Above: **Karstadt Mülheim.** First-floor plan

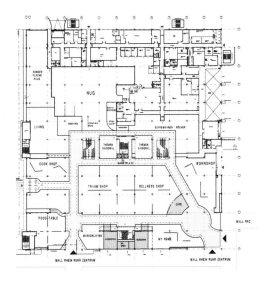

Above: **Karstadt Mülheim.** Ground-floor plan

Rei Kawakubo with
Elise Capdenat, Vedovamazzei,
Michael Howells and Jan de Cock

Dover Street Market

London 2004

Dover Street Market is a 1,200-square-metre enterprise split over six floors in a stately old red-brick building in Mayfair. Run by Comme des Garçons, it is much more than a boutique outlet for the brand, and is in fact a department store selling a myriad of other luxury brands, such as John Galliano, that carry the similar luxury-meets-radical ethic that has been the mainstay of the firm. Of course, the label refrains from describing the shop as a department store, which has become a sullied term associated with low expectations. 'Market' is more alive with possibilities and it suits the rough and ready premise of the concept. Rei Kawakubo, the mastermind of Comme des Garçons, is herself responsible for the overall design, and opened the store with a mission statement that reveals that she was looking for the 'accidental' when she devised the premise: 'I wanted to create a kind of market where various creators from various fields gather together and encounter each other in an ongoing atmosphere of beautiful chaos.' The design continually counterbalances finesse with unfinished and rough surfaces, and humorously plays with expectations of form, texture and materials.

The design is fluid and relies on curation, blending the products with the sort of installations one would expect in a radical art gallery. There is a constant collision between different aesthetics, designed to throw expectations off kilter and allow for the opportunity of new narratives. This is helped by Kawakubo's decision to work with different artists and designers for each floor. The ground floor has involved the artists Vedovamazzei and sets out many of the unifying motifs of the design. The customers are greeted by rough concrete flooring that immediately creates a contrast with the historical serenity of the building, as does the grey-panelled modular ceiling that incorporates lighting and air-conditioning vents in the style of an unappealing office block. Beautiful wooden and glass jewellery display cabinets rub shoulders with an octagonal, unpainted plywood perfume display in the shape of a funnel, all set against the backdrop of exposed, rough brick walls. The service desk is set within a rusting corrugated shed, held together with reused wooden planks, while a library section features a glass display tabletop, though the sense of luxury is undermined by the unpainted MDF table it sits on. Also on the first floor, a men's clothing section is held within a metal, Meccano-like frame that has been roughly painted orange. Inside, the changing room is the type of WC unit found on a construction site, but this one is painted a high-gloss red-orange. The theme is the marriage of construction and deconstruction, a paradox that enthuses the Comme des Garçons brand.

In the basement, designed along with the fourth floor by theatre designer Elise Capdenat, deconstruction seems to be getting the upper hand. The grey ceiling panels have been removed, leaving just a grid that holds the lighting and air-conditioning components and reveals a metal ceiling. In one area there are smoothed concrete partition walls with cut-through oval holes, revealing other parts of the store or storage areas. Trunks are used as display cases and the shell of a brown horse, almost life-size and cut in half lengthways, makes a dominant, peculiar sculpture. Exposure may have been taken to another level, but there are also soft touches like the funereal dried-flower arrangement that hangs above upright wooden display cabinets stacked with folded clothing.

The first and third floors are by film-set designer Michael Howells. For the first floor, Kawakubo set the theme of 'Shakespeare meets Picasso'. Luxury and finish are often to be found on the inside of a partitioned section, rather than its exterior. For example, the changing room is an untreated MDF box, but inside is rather luxurious and expertly finished with cushioned wall panels. Unpainted wooden joists and hessian material frame one, perhaps Cubist-inspired, area, but inside the joists are hidden and the material is finished with pure white. The other side of the floor is more Shakespearean, while still maintaining the theme of exposure. An ornate painted archway indicates glamour, but a section of wood is cut through to reveal it as superficial, like a film or stage set. The walls are decorated with a lightning-streaked night sky, while slashed-black curtains add to the Gothic glamour. However, the hanging display of tubular scaffolding and another corrugated shed ensure that any sense of romance is curtailed.

Howells' third-floor design is based on a 'Cabaret' theme, and most notably features a dishevelled bed with a mannequin's shoe-clad foot sticking out from under the covers. A flatscreen television lies at an angle on the bed, expressing a collision of worlds. A huge, floor-to-ceiling, faded gilt birdcage, adorned with velvet curtains, has a mirror hanging from its centre, while Galliano areas features walls, boxes and a seat cover decorated with a newspaper called the *Galliano Express*. Once again, the threat of anarchy is present, this time in the form of partially boarded-up windows.

Opposite and below: Dover Street Market London. The first-floor design by Michael Howells, a film-set designer whose work includes *Bright Young Things* and *Nanny McPhee*, features Rei Kawakubo-designed black plastic chairs in a women's clothing display area. Curvaceous, hollow and 1950s futurist influenced, they stand before the building's original shuttered windows, creating a striking contrast

Right and below right: **Dover Street Market London.** In the basement, ovals are cut through smooth plaster walls and the changing room pod is more familiar as a construction-site toilet. A dried-flower display softens the theme of deconstruction

Above: **Dover Street Market London.** The octagonal plywood fragrance display on the ground floor, as seen from the library section, features an MDF and glass display table. Luxury and cheap materials sit cheek by jowl throughout the six floors

Right: **Dover Street Market London.** The second floor is designed by artist Jan de Cock. The entire ceiling is decorated with a series of suspended, open-ended boxes made of MDF and featuring a series of veneers. Boxes are also used for display, while the main display system is tubular scaffolding

Right: **Dover Street Market London.** Elise Capdenat's fourth-floor design features a pristine café area with stainless steel units and wooden box tables, and metal flooring. The café provides views of the variety of surrounding rooftops through a floor-to-ceiling window

Listings — Store Details

Alexander McQueen
www.alexandermcqueen.net

417 West 14th Street
New York
NY 10014
USA
Tel: +1 212 645 1797

Azzedine Alaïa

4 rue de Moussy
Paris 75004
France
Tel +33 (0)142 721919

Burberry
www.burberry.com

Via Verri
Milan 20121
Italy
Tel +39 (0)276 08201

Catriona MacKechnie
www.catrionamackechnie.com

400 West 14th Street
New York
NY 10014
USA
Tel +1 212 242 3200
Fax +1 212 242 3370

Chloe
www.chloe.com

Mandarin Oriental Hotel
5 Connaught Road
Central Hong Kong
Tel +852 (0) 2865 2833
Fax +852 (0) 2865 6336

152–3 Sloane Street
London SW1X 9BX
UK
Tel +44 (0)20 782 35348

850 Madison Avenue
New York
NY 10021
USA
Tel +1 212 717 8220

Comme des Garçons
16 Place Vendôme
Paris 75001
France
Tel +33 (0)147 036090

5–2–1 Minamiaoyama
Minato-ku
Tokyo 107
Japan
Tel + 81 (0)3 406 3951

116 Wooster Street
New York
NY 10012
USA
Tel +1 212 219 0660

Dover Street Market
www.doverstreetmarket.com

17–18 Dover Street
London W1S 4LT
UK
Tel +44 (0)20 7518 0680
Fax +44 (0)20 7518 0681

Emporio Armani
www.emporioarmani.com

Emporio Armani/Chater
House
11 Chater Road
Central
Hong Kong SAR
Tel +852 (0)2532 7711
Fax +852 (0)2532 7719

Fendi
www.fendi.com

24 Rue François 1er
Paris 7500
France
Tel +33 (0)149 528452
Fax +33 (0)149 529868

36–40 Via Borgognona
Rome 00187
Italy
Tel +39 (0)669 6661
Fax +39 (0)669 940808

20–2 Sloane Street
London SW1X 9NE
UK
Tel +44 (0)20 7838 6288
Tel +44 (0)20 7838 6289

Galaxie Lafayette
www.galerieslafayette.de

Galeries Lafayette
Fransösischestrasse 23
Berlin 10117
Germany
Tel +49 (0)30 2094 8112
Fax +49 (0)30 2094 8214

Gianfranco Ferré
www.gianfrancoferre.com

9 Via Sant Andrea
Milan 20121
Italy
Tel. +39 (0)279 4864

Giorgio Armani
www.giorgioarmani.com

2093 Rua Bela Cinta
Cerquiera Cesar
São Paulo 01415–002
Brazil
Tel. +55 (0)11 3062 2660
Fax. +55 (0)11 3897 9071

6 Place Vendôme
Paris 75001
France
Tel. +33 (0)142 615509
Fax. +33 (0)140 150731

9 Via Sant Andrea
Milan 20121
Italy
Tel. +39 (0)276 003234
Fax +39 (0)276 014926
37 Sloane Street

London SW1X 9LP
UK
Tel. +44 (0)20 7235 6232
Fax. +44 (0)20 7823 1342

Hermès
www.hermes.com

4-1 Ginza 5-chome
Chuo-ku
Tokyo 104–0061
Japan
Tel +81 (0)3 3289 6811
Fax +81 (0)3 3289 6812

Jil Sander
www.jilsander.com

32-4 Osterfeldstrasse
Hamburg 22529
Germany
Tel +49 (0)40 553 02 0
Fax +49 (0)40 553 30 34

11 East 57th Street
New York
NY 10022
USA
Tel +1 212 8386100

Karstadt
www.karstadt.de

Rhein-Ruhr-Zentrum
5 Humboldtring
Mülheim 45472
Germany
Tel +49 (0)208 49510

Longchamp
www.longchamp.com

312 Spring Street
New York
NY 10012
USA
Tel +1 212 343 7444
Fax +1 212 343 7392

Lotte
www.lotteshopping.com

1 Sogong-dong
Jung-gu
Seoul 100-070
South Korea
Tel +82 (0)2 771 2500

Louis Vuitton
www.vuitton.com

22 Avenue Montaigne
Paris 75008
France
Tel +33 (0)810 810 010

Nagoya Sakae
3–16–17 Nishiki
Naka-ku
Nagoya 460-0003
Japan
Tel +81 (0)5 2957 3051

3–6–1 Ginza Chuo-Ku
Tokyo 104-8130
Japan
Tel +81 (0)3 3567 1211

Roppongi Keyakizaka Dori
Roppongi Hills
6–12–3 Roppongi Minato-ku
Tokyo 106-0032
Japan
Tel +81 (0)3 3478 2100

99–18 Chungdam-Dong
Kangnam-Ku
Seoul 135-100
Korea
Tel +82 (0)2 548 21 65
Fax +82 (0)2 548 21 62

116 Greene Street
New York NY 10012
USA
Tel +1 212 274 9090
Fax +1 212 274 8789

Marni
www.marni.it

57 Avenue Montaigne
Paris 75008
France
Tel +33 (0)156 880808
70 Via Sismondi
Milan 20133
Italy
Tel +39 (0)270 005479
Fax +39 (0)271 040309

26 Sloane Street
London SW1X 9NE
UK
Tel +44 (0)20 7245 9520

161 Mercer St.
New York NY 10012
USA
Tel +1 212 343 3912

Martine Sitbon
89–20 Chungdam-Dong
Kangnam–ku
Seoul 135–100
South Korea
Tel + 82 2 542 0095

Missoni
www.missoni.com

8 Via Montenapoleone
Milan 20121
Italy
Tel +39 (0)276 003555
Fax +39 (0)276 021923

78 Piazza di Spagna
Rome 00187
Italy
Tel & Fax +39 (0)6 67 92555

1009 Madison Avenue
New York
NY 10021
USA
Tel +1 212 517 9339
Fax +1 212 439 6037

Nicole Farhi
www.nicolefarhi.com

10 East 60th Street
New York NY 10022
USA
Tel +1 212 223 8811

Oki-ni
www.okini.com

25 Savile Row
London W1S 3PR
UK
Tel +44 (0)207 494 1716

Paul Smith
www.paulsmith.co.uk

Palazzo Gallarati Scotti
30 Via Manzoni
Milan 20121
Italy
Tel +39 (0)276 319181

Westbourne House
122 Kensington Park Road
London W11 2EP
UK
Tel +44 (0)20 7727 3553

Pleats Please
www.pleatsplease.com

3 rue des Rosiers
Paris 75004
France
Tel +33 (0)140 299966

La Place de Minami Aoyama
3–13–21 Minami-Aoyama
Minato-ku
Tokyo 107-0062
Japan
Tel +81 (0)3 5772 7750

Prada
www.prada.com

5–2–6 Minami-Aoyama
Minato-ku
Tokyo 107-0062
Japan
Tel +81 (0)3 6418 0400

575 Broadway
New York NY 10012
USA
Tel +1 212 334-8888

Selfridges
www.selfridges.com

Upper Mall East
Bull Ring
Birmingham B5 4BP
UK
Tel +44 (0)8708 377377

Stella McCartney
www.stellamccartney.com

30 Bruton Street
London W1J 6LG
UK
Tel +44 (0)20 7518 3100

429 West 14th Street
New York NY 10014
USA
Tel +1 212 255 1556

Bibliography

Publications

Raul A Barreneche, *New Retail*, Phaidon Press (London), 2005

Neil Bingham, *The New Boutique: Fashion and Design*, Merrell Publishers Ltd (London), 2005

Antonello Boschi (editors), *Showrooms*, teNeues (Kempen), 2001

Helen Castle (editor), *Architectural Design - Fashion + Architecture*, Vol 70, No 6, 2000

Rasshied Din, *New Retail*, Conran Octopus Ltd (London), 2000

Dress Code – Interior Design for Fashion Shops, Frame Publishers (Amsterdam), 2006

Deborah Fausch, Paulette Singley, Rodolphe El-Khourj, Zvi Efrah (editors), *Architecture: In Fashion*, Princeton Architectural Press (New York), 1994

Inclusive: The Architecture of Louis Vuitton, 2003 (to accompany the exhibition 'Inclusive: 1 Brand, 6 Architects, 11 Projects', Berlin 2003), AedesBerlin (Berlin), 2003

Logique/Visuelle: The Architecture of Louis Vuitton 2003 (to accompany the exhibition 'Mathematique des Objets Sensibles' held at LV Hall and Tokyo International Forum April 2003), Louis Vuitton (Japan), 2003

Otto Riewoldt, *Retail Design*, Laurence King (London), 2000

Articles

Susie Boyt, 'Where You'll Shop Next', *Financial Times Weekend*, 31 August 2003, p W4

Grace Bradbury, 'The Gospel According to Paul Smith', *Evening Standard Magazine*, 13 February 2004, pp 26-9

'The Case for Brands', *The Economist*, 6 September 2001, seen at www.economist.com

'A Costly Luxury', *The Economist*, 6 February 2003, seen at www.economist.com

Ed Crooks and Susanna Voyke, 'Comment & Analysis: The mindset is one we haven't seen for quite a while: people are worried, there's a real reluctance to spend', *Financial Times*, 28 June 2003, seen at www.ft.com

'Don't Mix your Designers', *The Economist,* 14 January 1999, seen at www.economist.com

'Every Cloud Has a Satin Lining', *The Economist,* 21 March 2002, seen at www.economist.com

Mike Exon, 'New Blood Takes Bland Out of the Brand', *Financial Times – Creative Businesss section*, 10 June 2003, p 6

'Harvey Nichols Opens New Manchester Store', www.manchestercalling.com, 11 August 2003

Edwin Heathcote, 'Architecture: Theatrical Art of High Consumerism', *Financial Times*, 15 September 2003, seen at www.ft.com

Edwin Heathcote, 'Light. Nob. Felt. Things: A Chat with Tom Emerson', in Edwin Heathcote (guest editor), *Architectural Design – Furniture + Architecture*, Vol 72, No 4, 2002, p 72–7

Damian Foxe, 'All About Yves – and Gucci', *Financial Times Weekend*, 20–1 September 2003, p W6

Mark Irving, 'Being Miuccia', *Financial Times Magazine*, 21 June 2003, p 25

'It's shopping but not as we know it', *Marks and Spencer Magazine*, Spring 2004

Craig Kellogg, 'The Matchmaker', in Neil Spiller (guest editor), *Architectural Design – Reflective Architecture*, Vol 72, No 3, 2002, p 98–101

Troy McMullen, 'Louis Vuitton Brands Its Space', *Wall Street Journal*, 13–15 June 2003, p A8

Daniela Mecozzi, 'Selling Style', *Frame*, Vol 30, January-February 2003, seen at www.framemag.com

'Prada Flagship Store, New York', www.galinsky.com

'Radice's Relaxed Vision for Future of M&S', *The Observer*, 25 May 2003, seen at observer/guardian.co.uk

Fiona Rattray, 'Hard Sell', *The Independent*, 27 January 2004, seen at www.independent.co.uk

Paula Reed, 'Daddy Bare', *Observer Food Monthly*, January 2004, p 49–51

'Reinventing the Store', *The Economist* – Special Report on Retail, 22 November 2003, p 89

Stella Shamoon, 'My Gamble with Gucci', *The Mail On Sunday – Financial Mail section*, 1 February 2004, p 7

'When Profits Go Out of Fashion', *The Economist,* 3 July 2003, seen at www.economist.com

Journals

L'Arca, September 2003

Frame, July–August 2003

Architectural Record, September 2003

Harpers & Queen, July 2003

Icon, September 2003

Domus, July–August 2003

Lotus, edition 118, 2003

For Reference

Not to be taken from this room